M. ARMSTRONG
IMP

AFF

AFFIRMING YOUR FAITH

EXPLORING THE APOSTLES' CREED

ALISTER McGRATH

Inter-Varsity Press

INTER-VARSITY PRESS
38 De Montfort Street, Leicester LE1 7GP, England

First published 1991
Reprinted 1991

British Library Cataloguing in Publication Data
McGrath, Alister E. (Alister Edgar), 1953–
Affirming your faith.
1. Apostles' Creed
I. Title
238.11

ISBN 0-85110-854-7

Set in Linotype Baskerville

Typeset in Great Britain by Parker Typesetting Service

Printed and bound in Great Britain by
Cox & Wyman Ltd, Reading, Berkshire

Inter-Varsity Press is the book-publishing division of the Universities and Colleges Christian Fellowship (formerly the Inter-Varsity Fellowship), a student movement linking Christian Unions in universities and colleges throughout the United Kingdom and the Republic of Ireland, and a member movement of the International Fellowship of Evangelical Students. For information about local and national activities write to UCCF, 38 De Montfort Street, Leicester LE1 7GP.

Contents

The Apostles' Creed

I believe in God, the Father almighty, Creator of heaven and earth. I believe in Jesus Christ, his only Son, our Lord. He was conceived by the power of the Holy Spirit, and born of the Virgin Mary. He suffered under Pontius Pilate, was crucified, died and buried. He descended to the dead. On the third day he rose again. He ascended into heaven, and is seated at the right hand of the Father. He will come again to judge the living and the dead. I believe in the Holy Spirit, the holy catholic church, the communion of saints, the forgiveness of sins, the resurrection of the body, and the life everlasting. Amen.

Introduction

MANY Christians are aware of the need to deepen their understanding of the gospel. Those who have come to faith recently often want someone to help them understand more about Christianity. But older Christians often feel the same need, aware of their lack of knowledge and understanding of key areas of their faith. The existence of countless Christian study groups, meeting in homes and churches throughout the world, points to this need. The problem with many Christian study groups, however, is that they often have difficulty in deciding what to study! They have problems setting their agendas. There are, in fact, few better subjects for such groups to study than the Apostles' Creed. It provides a neat summary of many of the main points of the Christian faith. And it is already familiar to many Christians, who are accustomed to using it during the course of Sunday worship.

This book is intended as a study guide to the Apostles' Creed. Whether you are studying on your own, or in a group, I hope that this work will help you think through some areas of your faith, and deepen your understanding of what you believe. Faith is indeed something which is 'caught, not taught' – but there is more to faith than trusting in God. A faith which remains at this level will be immature and superficial, vulnerable to doubt and of little use in evangelism. It is difficult to explain Christianity to an outsider if you haven't thought about it much yourself. Christians do indeed trust in God – but they believe certain quite definite things about him, and the impact this must have upon us as believers. The Apostles' Creed is an ideal starting point for this vital process of consolidating your grasp of your faith.

The meaning of the word 'creed'

Many words in the English language owe their origins to Latin. This is especially true of words relating to Christianity. For more than a thousand years, Latin was the language of educated Christians. It isn't surprising that quite a few English words come from Latin. A good example is 'Maundy Thursday', the day immediately before Good Friday, when Christians traditionally focus their thoughts on the Last Supper. In the Middle Ages, church services were invariably held in Latin, and the text chosen to begin the celebration of the Last Supper was John 13:34, 'A new command I give you: Love one another. As I have loved you, so you must love one another.' In Latin, these words began *mandatum novum do vobis* .... The English word 'Maundy' derives from the first Latin word spoken at that service – *mandatum*, 'a commandment'.

Exactly the same thing can be seen to have happened with the English word 'creed'. For more than a thousand years, Christians in western Europe knew the Creed only in Latin. Its opening words are *credo in Deum*, 'I believe in God.' Many will be familiar with these Latin words, or some very similar to them, from the choral works of composers such as Bach, Haydn, Mozart or Beethoven. The English word 'creed' derives from that word *credo*. As the word suggests, it is a statement of faith. It is an attempt to summarize the main points of what Christians believe. It is not exhaustive; nor is it meant to be.

The origins of the creeds

The origins of the Apostles' Creed may be found within the New Testament itself. There are frequent calls to be 'baptized in the name of Jesus Christ' (Acts 2:38; 8:12; 10:48), or 'in the name of the Lord Jesus' (Acts 8:16, 19:5). In its simplest form, the earliest Christian creed seems to have been simply 'Jesus is Lord!' (Romans 10:9; 1 Corinthians 12:3; 2 Corinthians 4:5; Philippians 2:11). Anyone who made this declaration was regarded as being a Christian. The Christian is one who 'receives Jesus Christ as Lord' (Colossians 2:6). It is a powerful statement to make, as it involves two related claims. In the first place, it declares the believer's loyalty and commitment to Jesus Christ. As we shall see, for someone to confess that 'Jesus Christ is Lord' is to declare that Jesus is the Lord of his or her life. To recognize that Jesus is Lord is to seek to do his will. The refusal of the first Christians to worship the Roman emperor reflects this belief: you can only serve one master, and for the Christian that is, and must be, none other than Jesus himself. In the second place, 'Jesus is Lord' declares certain things about Jesus, especially his relation to God.

As time went on, however, it became necessary to explain what Christians believed in more detail. The full implications of declaring that 'Jesus is Lord' needed to be teased out. What did Christians believe about God? about Jesus? about the Holy Spirit? By the fourth century, the Apostles' Creed as we now know it had assumed a more or less fixed form; what variations did exist were slight, and were finally eliminated in the seventh century. The Apostles' Creed is a splendid summary of the apostolic teaching concerning the gospel, even though it was not actually written by the apostles.

When someone became a Christian in the early church, great emphasis was placed on the importance of his or her baptism. During the period of Lent (the period from Ash Wednesday to Easter), those who had recently come to faith were given instruction in Christian beliefs. Finally, when they had mastered the basics of faith, they would recite the Creed together, as a corporate witness to the faith in which they believed – and which they now understood. Faith had been reinforced with understanding. They would then be baptized with great ceremony and joy on Easter Day itself, as the church celebrated the resurrection of its Lord and Saviour. In this way, the significance of the baptism of the believer could be fully appreciated: he or she had passed from death to life (Romans 6:3–10). Baptism was a public demonstration of the believer's death to the world, and being born to new life in Jesus Christ.

A central part of the baptism celebration was the public declaration of faith by each candidate. Anyone who wished to be baptized had to declare publicly his or her faith in Jesus Christ. At many times in the history of the Christian church, this was exceptionally dangerous: to admit to being a Christian could mean imprisonment, victimization, suffering, or even death. (The English word 'martyr', incidentally, derives from the Greek word meaning 'witness'. To be a martyr was seen as the finest witness possible to Jesus Christ and his gospel.) The believer did not, however, merely recite a creed; he or she was also asked, as an individual, whether he or she *personally* believed in the gospel, before he or she could be baptized. Here is part of a sermon preached in the fourth century to those who had just been baptized, in which this practice is described. (Incidentally, note the important references to Romans 6:3–4; those who have died to their past have risen to new life in Christ.)

> You were asked, 'Do you believe in God the father almighty?' You replied, 'I believe', and were immersed, that is, were buried. Again, you were asked, 'Do you believe in our Lord Jesus Christ and his cross?' You replied, 'I believe', and were immersed. Thus you were buried with Christ, for he who is buried with Christ rises again with him. A third time you were asked, 'Do you believe in the Holy Spirit?' You replied, 'I believe', and were immersed for a third time. Your three-fold confession thus wiped out the many sins of your previous existence.

Historically, then, the Creed was the profession of faith made by converts at their baptism, and formed the basis of their instruction. As more and more individuals now come to discover Christianity as adults, the Creed can once more serve this historic purpose. It is thus an ideal subject for a 'nurture group'.

The Apostles' Creed, however, was not the only creed to come into existence in the period of the early church. Two major controversies in the early church made it necessary to be more precise about certain matters of doctrine. The first controversy (the Arian controversy of the fourth century) centred on the relationship of Jesus and God. In order to avoid inadequate understandings of the relation of the Father and Son, the Council of Chalcedon (451 AD) endorsed a creed now generally known as the 'Nicene Creed'. This creed, roughly twice as long as the Apostles' Creed, begins with the words 'We believe in one God.' In its efforts to insist upon the reality of the divinity of Jesus Christ, this creed speaks of Jesus as 'being of one substance with the Father'.

A second major controversy centred on the doctrine of the Trinity. In order to avoid inadequate understandings of the relation of the Father, Son and Spirit, the 'Athanasian Creed' was drawn up. This creed, which opens with the words 'Whoever wishes to be saved...', is by far the longest of the three creeds, and is nowadays rarely used in any form of public worship.

Our attention, however, concerns the Apostles' Creed, which is the oldest and simplest creed of the church. All Christian churches recognize its authority and its importance as a standard of doctrine. To study the Apostles' Creed is to investigate a central element of our common Christian heritage. It is an affirmation of the basic beliefs which unite

Christians throughout the world and across the centuries.

The purpose of the creeds

As we have seen, the creeds had their origins as a profession or confession of faith made by converts at their baptism. Since then, they have served other purposes – for example, as a test of orthodoxy for Christian leaders, or as an act of praise in Christian worship. In our own day and age, the creeds serve three main purposes.

In the first place, the creeds provide *a brief summary of the Christian faith.* A creed is not, and was never meant to be, a substitute for personal faith: it attempts to give substance to a personal faith which already exists. You do not become a Christian by reciting a creed; rather, it provides a useful summary of the main points of your faith. There are certain items which are not dealt with. For example, there is no section which states 'I believe in Scripture'. This isn't necessary, in that the Creed is basically a distillation or summary of the main points of the scriptural teaching concerning the gospel. The importance of the Bible is assumed throughout; indeed, most of the Creed can be shown to consist of direct quotations from Scripture.

It is quite possible that some of the components of the Creed may seem a little strange or unfamiliar to those who have come to faith recently. Don't be alarmed by this: it is just a gentle reminder that there is more to Christianity than you think at this stage. As you grow, you'll begin to appreciate the wisdom of including material, for example, on the church, which often seems out of place to young Christians.

This brings us neatly on to the second purpose served by the creeds: to allow us to *recognize and avoid inadequate or incomplete versions of Christianity*. Some people, for example, might insist that Christianity is mainly (or perhaps even entirely) about the Holy Spirit. Others might reject this angrily, replying that Christianity is primarily about God the Father. The Apostles' Creed reminds us that there is much more to the gospel than either of these. By providing a balanced and biblical approach to the Christian faith, tried and tested by believers down the centuries, the Creed allows us to recognize deficient versions of the gospel. For example, the two views cited above make no reference to Jesus himself, which is a serious omission. They are not *wrong*; they are just *inadequate*. Many people have found their faith immeasurably strengthened and matured by being forced to think through areas of faith which they would otherwise not have explored. See the Creed as an invitation to explore and discover areas of the gospel, which otherwise you might miss or overlook. For example, many evangelicals are individualists, who have no real sense of belonging to a community. The Creed's affirmation of belief in the church reminds us of the corporate dimension of faith, and helps correct any unhealthy individualism.

Many people who have come to faith recently want to be baptized, in order to make a public declaration of their faith. A central part of that celebration of your new birth will probably be the congregation declaring their corporate faith, using the words of the Apostles' Creed. Let that be a stimulus to you! See the Creed as setting the agenda for your personal exploration of the Christian faith.

See it as mapping out areas for you to explore, on your own or with others. Some of its statements may remind you of those ancient maps, where vast areas of the world were marked as '*terrae incognitae*, unknown territory'. But see this as a challenge! It may take you some time to fathom the depths of your faith – but there is no rush. I hope that this book may help you begin to explore your faith, as you travel further down the road of faith.

In the third place, the creeds emphasize that *to believe is to belong*. To become a Christian is to enter a community of faith, which stretches right back to the upper room (John 21). By putting your faith in Jesus Christ, you have become a member of his body, the church, which used this Creed to express its faith. By studying it, you are reminding yourself of the many men and women who have used it before you. It gives you a sense of history and perspective. It emphasizes that you are not the only person to put your trust in Jesus Christ. Think of how many others recited those words at their baptism down the centuries. Think of how many others found in the Apostles' Creed a statement of their personal faith. You share that faith, and you can share the same words that they used to express it.

How to use this book

You will find it helpful to notice three things about this book.

1. The Creed has been broken down into sixteen sections, each of which is suitable for an evening's study. Every effort has been made to keep each chapter the same length. Don't let my division of the material get in your way! If you feel you need more

time to study a section, then spread it out over two If you feel I have spent too long over a couple of sections, then merge them into a single evening's study. Please be flexible, and do not let the structure of this book inhibit you. It isn't meant to be a rigid strait-jacket.

2. Wherever possible, each chapter attempts to explore the biblical foundations of the Creed, to deal with some common difficulties which are often encountered, to explain ideas which some find confusing, and to demonstrate the relevance of these beliefs to everyday life. Sadly, pressure on space often makes it impossible to do this properly. It is hoped, however, that you will find some of the ideas and illustrations helpful.

3. Each chapter ends with the same three sections: first, some *key scriptural passages* are noted, to allow you to explore the scriptural foundations of the section of the Creed being examined; second, some *questions for discussion* are identified, in order to assist groups to follow up particular points of interest; third, some suggestions are made *for further reading*, to allow you to follow up matters in greater depth, should this seem appropriate. I hope that this regular pattern will not merely make this book easier to read, but also that it may help give structure to group discussions.

For further reading

Gerald Bray, *Creeds, Councils and Christ*, pp. 92–118. A concise introduction to the history of the creeds, and the background against which they are to be set.

Henry Chadwick, *The Early Church*. An eminently

readable account of the spread of Christianity, with much useful background material to the history of the creeds.

J. N. D. Kelly, *Early Christian Creeds*. An invaluable historical introduction to the development of the creeds in the early church.

CHAPTER ONE

I believe

THE Creed opens with a powerful assertion: 'I believe'. It is an assertion which is repeated three times during the course of the Creed. What does it mean?

The idea explained

1. *Faith means assent.* Faith is believing that certain things are true. 'I believe in God' means something like 'I believe that there is a God', or 'I am of the opinion that God exists'. Faith assents to the existence of God. It affirms a belief in the existence of God. This is an essential starting point. After all, before we can begin to say anything about what God is like, we need to assume that there is a God in the first place. Many people outside the Christian faith, however, assume that there is nothing more to Christian faith than assent to God's existence. For such people, 'I believe in God' has roughly the same status as 'I believe in fairies.' For them, faith is just assent to a list of propositions. There is nothing more to Christian belief than running through a checklist of propositions – such as those contained in the Creed itself.

It is very easy to see how this totally inadequate and misleading idea of faith arises. In part, the chief culprit is the English language. In the introduction, we noted that the Creed was originally written in Latin, and that its first words – *credo in Deum* – are traditionally translated as 'I believe in God.' This is only one of several possible ways of translating the word. Other, more reliable translations would be 'I have confidence in God', 'I put my trust in God', or simply 'I trust in God.' The English translation 'I believe in God' could just mean 'I am of the opinion that there is a God', when in fact it is meant to be a much stronger statement – 'I put my trust in God.' I am certainly of the opinion that God exists – but there is more to faith than this!

2. *Faith means trust.* When I declare that 'I believe in Jesus Christ', I am not just saying that there once was a man called Jesus. I am affirming my trust in him. Faith cannot be equated with knowing. It is not something cold and cerebral, enlightening the mind while leaving the heart untouched. Faith is the response of our whole persons to the person of God. It is a joyful reaction on our part to the overwhelming divine love we see revealed in Jesus Christ. It is the simple response of leaving all to follow Jesus. Faith is both our recognition that something wonderful has happened through the life, death and resurrection of Jesus Christ, and our response to what has happened. Faith realizes that God loves us, and responds to that love. Faith is saying 'Yes' to God. It is a *decision*, an *act of will* to trust God.

Christians don't just *believe* – we believe *in someone*. Faith is like an anchor, linking us with the object of faith. Just as an anchor secures a ship to the ocean floor, so our faith links us securely with God. Faith is not just believing that God exists; it is about anchoring ourselves to that God, and resting secure in doing so. Whatever storms life may bring, the anchor of faith will hold us firm to God.

Perhaps the clearest exposition of this aspect of faith may be found in Hebrews 11:1 – 12:3. This famous passage opens with a definition of faith (11:1) as 'being sure of what we hope for and certain of what we do not see'. What this means is illustrated by the trust of the individuals mentioned in the remainder of the chapter. Abraham was called to go to a strange land to receive his inheritance (11:8) – and he trusted God, and went. All believed that God could be trusted, and acted on the basis of that faith. This great passage closes (12:1–3) by urging us to consider all these great men and women of faith, to learn from their example, and to trust God as they did.

3. *Faith means commitment.* It is helpful to remember the close links between the Creed and baptism in the early church. When Christian converts declared that they believed in God, in Jesus Christ, and in the Holy Spirit, they were declaring publicly their commitment to the gospel. They were not just telling the world *what* they believed about Jesus Christ; they were telling the world *that* they believed in Jesus Christ. 'I believe in God' means 'I have committed myself to God.' To believe in God is to belong to God.

Time and time again, Scripture encourages us to think of our faith as a personal relationship with God. God is one who has publicly demonstrated his commitment to and love for us in the cross of Jesus Christ; he will not abandon us. He will be with us, wherever we go. Faith is our commitment to God,

relied upon him. People like this were called 'half-way' believers in eighteenth-century America. They are on their way to faith – but they have yet to arrive. For such people, 'I believe in God' can mean little more than 'I think there may be a God somewhere.' The richness and depth of the gospel remains something unknown to them.

Do you see yourself portrayed here? Is this you? If so, the remainder of this book will become a lot more interesting and relevant if you allow your faith to become personal trust in God. You may be like John Wesley, who believed that God could forgive sins, but had yet to know the heart-warming experience of having his own sins forgiven. For Wesley before his conversion, God forgave other people's sins; afterwards, he knew that his own sins had been forgiven.

Suppose you developed blood poisoning. Penicillin is an antibiotic which can cure this ailment. But believing that penicillin *can* cure your blood poisoning isn't enough to cure you. It is only by taking capsules of the substance that you can be cured. So it is with the gospel. Believing it can transform your life is one thing; allowing it to do just that is something else.

Key scriptural passages

Matthew 9:20–22; 27–30; Hebrews 11:1 – 12:3; James 2:14–24. See also Psalm 96:10–17; 99:1–5; Ezekiel 33:11–16; Luke 11:1–4; Philippians 3:13–14.

Questions for discussion

How would you distinguish these four terms: faith, belief, creed, gospel?

How do faith and doubt relate to each other?

How would you help (1) a non-Christian, and (2) a 'half-way' believer to come to faith?

Have you experienced your faith acting as an 'anchor' during a particularly stormy time?

For further reading

Alister McGrath, *Doubt*, pp. 9–39. A careful discussion of the relation of faith and doubt.

Os Guinness, *Doubt*. A valuable discussion of the relation of faith and doubt, although difficult reading at points.

C H A P T E R T W O

God, the Father almighty

WITH these words, we come to the first article of the Creed. Christians, we are told, believe in God. The two chapters which follow deal with the main points affirmed by the Creed.

The ideas explained

1. *God.* When the Creed speaks of God, it means 'the God and Father of our Lord Jesus Christ' (1 Peter 1:3). It is not dealing with some philosophical ideas of God, but the God who revealed himself in Scripture, and supremely in Jesus Christ. It is not referring to some *abstract idea* about God, but to the living and personal God whom Christians worship and adore.

Of course, this causes difficulties for some people. 'There isn't a god!', they argue. It is important to note that this is actually a statement of faith, rather than fact. What they really mean is 'I believe that there is no god' – which is as much a statement of faith as the Christian belief that there *is* a God! More generally, it must be noted that there are no arguments which establish either that God definitely exists, or that he definitely does not exist. Reason runs into difficulties when trying to cope with God. Tennyson made this point perfectly in his poem *The Ancient Sage*:

For nothing worthy proving can be proven,
Nor yet disproven.

Belief in God, it need hardly be added, rests upon solid foundations – even if paradoxically, as Tennyson suggests, it cannot be proved. Atheists and Christians alike take their positions as matters of faith. The former may like to try and represent their position as objective and scientific, but it is actually nothing of the sort.

Modern Western culture is going through a phase which is not just non-Christian, but actually anti-Christian. That means you must be realistic about the hostile attitudes against Christianity which you are likely to encounter. This has no bearing on whether Christianity is right or wrong. People may ridicule your faith in God – but that doesn't mean it is wrong. They may make you feel stupid or isolated on account of your faith in God; if they do, make sure you are supported by fellowship with other Christians. Join study or prayer groups, and draw comfort from the presence of other Christians. Encourage each other by your faith (Romans 1:12).

2. *Father*. Any idea of God as an impersonal being or force is immediately discounted by speaking of God as 'Father'. The Lord's Prayer is perhaps the most well-known example of God being addressed in this way (Matthew 6:9), although the use of 'Abba' is even more intimate (Mark 14:36; Romans 8:15; Galatians 4:6). But what does it mean to speak about God in this way?

Throughout Scripture, we find analogies which

point to God's ability to reveal himself in ways which we can understand. The scriptural images of God (for example, as Shepherd, King and Father) are deceptively simple. They are easy to visualize and remember, yet on further reflection, they convey important and profound truths concerning God. The doctrine of the incarnation points to God's willingness and ability to come down to our level. God reveals himself in ways appropriate to our level and our abilities as human beings, using illustrations which we can handle.

Analogies are memorable. They are powerful visual images, which stimulate our imagination. They get us thinking about God. Talking about God in abstract terms can get very boring and unimaginative. We all know that a picture is worth a thousand words. It is certainly correct to talk about God as one who cares for us, guides us, and accompanies us throughout life. But it is much more memorable to talk about God as a shepherd – an analogy which makes all those points! People can remember the idea of God as a shepherd, linking it with key scriptural passages (like Psalm 23). And as they think about those images, they can begin to unpack the various ideas which they convey.

The statement 'God is our Father' means that God is *like* a human father. In other words, God is analogous to a father. In some ways he is like a human father, and in others he is not. There are genuine points of similarity. God cares for us, as human fathers care for their children (note Matthew 7:9–11). God is the ultimate source of our existence, just as our fathers brought us into being. Just as there is something of our own fathers in each of us, so we are made in the image of our heavenly Father

(Genesis 1:26–27). God exercises authority over us, as do human fathers. He knows all our weaknesses and problems, as do human fathers. Equally, there are genuine points of dissimilarity. Speaking of God as 'Father' does not mean that God is a human being, for example! Nor does the necessity of a human mother point to the need for a divine mother.

God reveals himself in images and ideas which tie in with our world of everyday existence – yet which do not reduce God to that everyday world. When we say that 'God is our Father', we don't mean that he is just yet another human father! Rather, we mean that thinking about human fathers helps us think about God. They are analogies. Like all analogies, they break down at points. However, they are still extremely useful and vivid ways of thinking about God.

For some, however, thinking about God as a father is thoroughly unhelpful. They may have only negative memories of their fathers as tyrants. Their fathers may have abandoned them and their mothers at an early age. An image which is meant to convey compassion, care and commitment thus suggests quite the opposite. If this is a problem for you, perhaps the following brief thoughts may be helpful.

First, notice how often Scripture compares God to a human mother. The love of God for his people is often compared to the love of a mother for her child (*e.g.* Isaiah 49:15; 66:13). If you have fond memories of your mother, you may find it helpful to draw on these in thinking about God's care for you. Second, the analogy of God as Father also indicates what human fathers *ought* to be like. The same care, compassion and commitment which God shows towards us is meant to be reflected in the attitude of human fathers towards their children. Finally, remember that the best way of all of thinking about God is to think about Jesus Christ himself. 'Who has seen me has seen the Father' (John 14:9). Think of the love, care, and kindness you see reflected in the face of Jesus himself. *That* is what the love of God for you is like.

3. *Almighty*. This word causes problems for some. Does it mean that God can do *anything*, like make a triangle with four sides? Or that he can suddenly change his nature, and reject those who come to him in faith and repentance? While it can be fun to explore the logical niceties of these ideas, they aren't of much relevance to the real points at issue! Let's look at some of the points being made.

First, we are reminded that all power and authority in this world derive from God. Rulers, governments and Christian leaders all derive authority from God (Romans 13:1–2), and are responsible to him for the manner in which they exercise it. If you are a Christian leader (or think you might become one), let this be a sobering thought.

Second, we are reminded that things which seem impossible to us are perfectly possible for God. Remember Gabriel's gentle chiding of Mary, as she expressed astonishment that she was to bear the Saviour of the world: 'Nothing is impossible with God' (Luke 1:38). It is very easy for us to underestimate God; the Creed reminds us that he is able to do far more than we imagine.

Finally, remember that 'almighty' does not mean capricious or whimsical. Scripture stresses the *reliability* of God; having made a promise, God stands by it (Psalm 19:7–10). The Old Testament idea of a covenant – that is, a kind of bond or contract – between God and Israel made this same point: God has committed himself to us, in word and deed. The fact that he is almighty doesn't mean that he can or will suddenly change his mind about this! In his power and wisdom, God has chosen to achieve our salvation, and has committed himself to us in this way.

The ideas applied

Thinking about God as Father is particularly helpful in relation to prayer (Matthew 7:9–11). Human fathers, despite their weaknesses and shortcomings, wish the best for their children. So it is with God. But every now and then, a child may ask its father for something which is totally inappropriate – for example, a pump-action shotgun. The father's failure to give this to the child does not mean that he did not hear the request. It does not mean that he has ceased to care for the child. Rather, it means that his care and concern for the well-being of the child (and others in the neighbourhood!) prevents him from fulfilling that request. He may give something else instead – something more helpful and appropriate this time! Perhaps we could say that God answers the prayers which we *ought* to have prayed!

Key scriptural passages

Psalm 105:8–11; Matthew 6:9–13; 7:9–11; John 14:5–14; Romans 8:13–17.

Questions for discussion

What reasons would you give for believing in God?

What ideas does 'God as Father' suggest to you?

Is the idea of a *faithful* God contradicted by the idea of an *almighty* God?

For further reading

R. T. France, *The Living God*. A valuable guide to the scriptural understanding of God.

Alister McGrath, *Doubt*, pp. 9–47; 93–106. A helpful discussion of difficulties some feel in relation to believing in God.

Alister McGrath, *Understanding the Trinity*, pp. 45–77. A useful discussion of scriptural pictures of God, including God as Father.

J. I. Packer, *Knowing God*. A minor classic, full of helpful insights into its subject.

CHAPTER THREE

Creator of heaven and earth

TO talk about God as 'our Father' is to speak of his authority and care – but it is also to speak of his creativity. We are here because God brought us into being.

The ideas explained

Everything which we see in the world was created by God and belongs to God. This thought in itself moves many people to praise God (*e.g.* Psalm 8:1–3; 19:1–6; Revelation 4:11). It is helpful to think of God as a master-builder (Job 38:4–7), or an artist at work on a masterpiece. The world reflects the wisdom, power and majesty of the God who brought it into being. 'Since the creation of the world God's invisible qualities – his eternal power and divine nature – have been clearly seen, being understood from what has been made' (Romans 1:20). Anyone who has walked at night under a star-studded sky, with tiny points of light suspended in the blackness of space, will appreciate the point that Paul is making (*cf.* Psalm 8). At times, the presence, power and majesty of a Creator God seem to be written into the fabric of his creation. It is almost as if God, like a master artist, signed his name upon his creation for all to see.

There is, however, a limit to what can be known about God from nature. For example, nature may tell us that there is a God, that he is the Creator, and that he is good and wise. But we need to know substantially more about God than this if we are to come to know and trust him! Christianity points to the biblical record culminating in Jesus Christ, especially in his death and resurrection, as the supreme demonstration of the existence and character of God. It is *here* that Christianity has always insisted that God is most reliably disclosed and revealed: it is *here* that he may be found. The biblical witness to God both confirms and extends any knowledge of God available from nature itself.

Scripture endorses these insights drawn from nature – for example, that God is the Creator, and that he is good and wise – and takes them further. There is a hymn by Isaac Watts which deserves to be known better than it is:

> The heavens declare thy glory, Lord!
> In every star thy wisdom shines;
> But when our eyes behold thy word,
> We read thy name in clearer lines.

The basic point being made is that the scriptural witness to God is consistent with and endorses what we already know, or think we know, by experience – and that it both states this more clearly, and develops it further. Scripture establishes a reliable framework for thinking and talking about God, which goes far beyond the very modest knowledge of God which it is possible to derive from nature. And Scripture constructs this framework around the central events to which it bears witness: the life, death and resurrection of Jesus Christ.

In affirming our faith in God as Creator, however, we do not mean that God created the universe many years ago, and then left it untended. He is not like some old-fashioned watchmaker who makes and winds up a clockwork watch, and then leaves it to run without any further attention. (This idea of a 'clockwork universe', which became popular in the eighteenth century, is usually referred to as 'deism'.) Rather, God exercises continual care over his creation (Psalm 104). God once created, and now sustains, all things through his word (Genesis 1:3; Hebrews 1:3).

The ultimate demonstration of God's continuing concern for and involvement with his creation is his act of redemption in Jesus Christ. The creation is the theatre in which the great drama of redemption is played out. In redeeming us, God entered into his world as one of us (John 1:14). The Creator entered his creation, in order to restore it. The prologue to John's gospel (John 1:1–18) makes it clear that the work of redemption is closely linked with that of creation. God does not abandon his creation after sin.

If thinking about God as Creator seems very abstract, look at the world – the beauty of spring flowers, or the splendour of the heavens. God made those. The Belgic Confession (1561), a Calvinist statement of faith which exercised particular influence in the Low Countries (to become particularly noted for their botanists and physicists), declared that nature is 'before our eyes as a most beautiful book in which all created things, whether great or small, are as letters showing the invisible things of God to us'. It is, however, very easy to think of creation as something very impersonal. That is why it is helpful to turn our eyes away from the world to ourselves, and recall that God made *us*. Martin Luther, the German reformer, wrote:

> I believe that God has created me and all that exists; that he has given me and still sustains my body and soul, all my limbs and my senses, my reason and all the faculties of my mind, together with food and clothing, house and home, family and possessions; that he provides me daily and abundantly with all the necessities of life, protects me from all danger and preserves me from all evil.

Believing in God as Creator means believing that God made each one of us.

Earlier, we drew an analogy between God and an artist. Just as an artist signs his works, so the hand of God is evident within his creation. And as we are the height of God's creation (what a sobering thought!), we might expect to find signs of the hand of God within ourselves. Scripture tells us that we have been made in the image or likeness of God (Genesis 1:26–27). This has several important consequences.

First, it means that there is some sort of affinity between God and human beings. The French writer Pascal put it like this: 'There is a God-shaped gap within us.' In other words, we have been created with an inbuilt capacity to relate to God. To fulfil our potential as human beings, we need to relate to God. We remain unsatisfied and unfulfilled until we enter into a relationship with the God who created and redeemed us. Augustine, writing in the early fifth century, put it like this: 'You made us for yourself, O Lord, and our hearts are restless until they find their rest in you.' Many writers have written poignantly of the human tragedy – of the sense of lostness, loneliness and isolation felt by many people. Christianity affirms that this situation can be transformed by entering into a personal relationship with the God who created the world and each one of us – and made us with a view to loving us.

Second, being made in the image of God reminds us that we belong to God. We are not our own masters. We have been bought by God at a price (1 Corinthians 6:19--20). We are his. This insight gives new meaning to Jesus' famous words, 'Give to Caesar what is Caesar's, and to God what is God's' (Matthew 22:21). Jesus has been asked whether the Jews ought to pay taxes. Jesus asks to be shown a coin, and asks whose image is stamped upon it. 'Caesar's', they replied (Matthew 22:15–21). Jesus then speaks the famous words 'Give to Caesar what is Caesar's, and to God what is God's.' Those words ought to make us think along the following lines: 'What is Caesar's, and what is God's? How can we tell? The coin was stamped with the image of Caesar; but what has been stamped with the image of God? *We* have been stamped with that image and likeness. God made *us* with his own image impressed upon us. Therefore we must give ourselves over to God, for we are his.' Recognition that we are created in the image of God amounts to a demand for commitment and obedience – or, as we saw in an earlier chapter (p. 20), to a demand for *faith*.

The ideas applied

Recognition that the world belongs to God has important consequences for understanding our own responsibilities within that world. We have been placed within God's creation to tend it and take care of it (Genesis 2:15). We may be superior to the remainder of that creation, and exercise authority over it (Psalm 8:4–8) – but we remain under the authority of God, and responsible to him for the way in which we treat his creation. We are the stewards, not the owners, of creation. We hold it in trust. There is a growing realization today that past generations have seriously abused that trust. They have exploited the creation and its resources. There is a real danger that we shall spoil what God so wonderfully created.

Fortunately, there has been a growing awareness recently of the need to take a more responsible attitude towards creation. Reflecting on our responsibilities as stewards of God's creation is the first step in undoing the harm done by past generations. It matters to God that vast areas of our world are made uninhabitable through nuclear or toxic chemical waste. It matters that the delicate balance of natural forces is disturbed by human carelessness. Sin affects the way we treat the environment as much as it does our attitude towards God, other people, and society as a whole. This article of the Creed is the basis of a new – and overdue – attitude towards creation.

Realizing that God is Creator of the world is also important in another respect. As we noted, many people feel frightened and lonely in the world. They are overwhelmed by the thought of the immensity of space. The stars in the night sky seem to emphasize the brevity and unimportance of human life. After all, those stars are billions of miles away, and become further from us with each moment that passes. The light from them now reaching us may have begun its journey centuries ago, long before we were born.

The doctrine of creation allows us to feel at home in the world. It reminds us that we, like the rest of creation, were fashioned by God. We are here because God wants us to be here. We are not alone, but are in the very presence of the God who made and owns everything. We are in the presence of a friend, who knows us and cares for us. Behind the apparently faceless universe lies a person. The stars in the night sky are then no longer symbols of despair, but of joy – the same God who made *them* also made *me*, and cares for me! They are even reminders of God's promises, and their fulfilment (Genesis 15:1–6).

Key scriptural passages

Genesis 1 – 2; Psalms 8, 19, 104; Isaiah 40:28–31; Romans 1:20; Revelation 4:11.

Questions for discussion

Is the thought that God is Creator reassuring or challenging?

Is there anywhere in God's creation where you find yourself especially aware of his presence? A particular place? A sight? A work of art? A person?

What responsibilities does our stewardship of creation place on us?

For further reading

James Houston, *I believe in the Creator*. An excellent introduction to the doctrine of creation.

P. E. Hughes, *The True Image*. An in-depth analysis of human nature and destiny, in the light of the doctrine of creation.

C. S. Lewis, *Mere Christianity*. A splendid work, studded with insights on the importance of the doctrine of creation.

Alister McGrath, *Understanding the Trinity*, pp. 28–44. Highly readable account of what we can know about God from the created order.

CHAPTER FOUR

Jesus Christ, his only Son

WITH these words, we come to the second major section of the Creed. Our attention now shifts to Jesus Christ, and brings us to the heart of the Christian faith.

The ideas explained

The focus of the Creed is the name and the relevance of Jesus Christ. It is generally thought that the Creed represents an expansion of a very simple and basic confession of faith: 'Jesus is Lord!' At the centre of the Christian faith lies the person of Jesus Christ.

The core of the Christian faith is a person, not a set of abstract ideas or beliefs. We must resist the temptation to speak about Christianity as if it were some form of 'ism', like Buddhism, Freudianism or Marxism. These are essentially abstract systems which have become detached from the person of their founder, and reduced simply to sets of ideas or doctrines. All that Marx did was to introduce them; they are now quite independent of him. The relationship between Jesus and Christianity is, however, quite different. To begin with, Buddha, Freud and Marx are all dead – yet Christianity knows its head as living and risen from the dead.

Christians have always insisted that there was something qualitatively different about Jesus, which sets him apart from all other religious teachers or thinkers. There is a vitally close connection between the person and the message of Jesus. It is what Jesus did, and the impact which he made on those who encountered him, which make his message important. From the very beginning, Christians realized that Jesus just could not be treated as an ordinary human being. In Jesus, the message and the messenger are one and the same. Jesus' message is given weight and status because of who we recognize Jesus to be.

The name 'Jesus Christ' needs some explanation. Strictly speaking, we ought to write it as 'Jesus the Christ'. 'Christ' is actually a title, rather than just a surname. The very name Jesus gives a clue to his importance: 'You are to give him the name Jesus, because he will save his people from their sins' (Matthew 1:21). The name Jesus literally means 'God saves.' That this name was fully justified is demonstrated by the New Testament accounts of his death and resurrection, and the new relationship between believers and God which became possible as a result.

In calling Jesus 'the Christ', the New Testament writers are pointing to Jesus as the long-awaited Messiah. (The word 'Christ' is the Greek version of the Hebrew word 'Messiah'. See John 1:41.) The Messiah was the long-awaited deliverer of the people of God, promised within the pages of the Old Testament. Although there were many understandings of what the coming of the Messiah would be like, many linked his coming with prophecies such as Malachi 3:1, which spoke of someone coming to prepare the way for the coming of the Lord. This prophecy was held to be fulfilled through the appearance of John the Baptist (Mark 1:1–8). Thus when Peter recognizes Jesus as 'the Christ, the Son of the living God' (Matthew 16:16), he is identifying Jesus with the long-awaited Messiah.

The term 'Messiah' literally means 'the anointed one' – in other words, someone who has been anointed with oil. This Old Testament practice indicated that the person anointed in this way was regarded as having been singled out by God as having special importance. Thus 1 Samuel 24:6 refers to the king as 'the Lord's anointed'. The basic sense of the word 'Messiah' could be said to be 'the divinely appointed King of Israel'. As time passed, the term gradually came to refer to a deliverer, himself a descendent of David, who would restore Israel to the golden age she enjoyed under the rule of David. It is for this reason that New Testament writers stress that Jesus was a descendent of David (*e.g.* Matthew 1:1–17; Romans 1:3).

What do Christians believe about Jesus Christ? It is certainly true that Jesus was a first-century Jew, who lived in Palestine in the reign of Tiberius Caesar, and who was executed by crucifixion under Pontius Pilate. The Roman historian Tacitus refers to Christians deriving their name from 'Christ, who was executed at the hands of the procurator Pontius Pilate in the reign of Tiberius'. The historical evidence for his existence is sufficient to satisfy all but those who are determined to believe that he didn't exist, whatever the evidence may be. But it is at this point that we must pause to reflect. The Christian faith certainly presupposes that Jesus existed as a real historical figure, and that he was crucified. Christianity is, however, most emphatically not about the mere facts that Jesus existed and was crucified. Christian faith is not just the assertion that a man called Jesus really existed!

The Creed explains why Jesus is of such central importance to the Christian faith. It identifies a number of key beliefs which allow us to understand why he matters so much to Christians. The first reason it identifies is that Jesus is the 'Son of God'. What might this mean?

In the Old Testament, this phrase is occasionally used to refer to angelic or supernatural persons (see Psalm 82:6; Job 38:7; Daniel 3:25). The Old Testament also refers to the coming Messiah as the 'Son of God' (2 Samuel 7:12–14; Psalm 2:7; Psalm 89:26–27). In the New Testament, the term is used to highlight the unique nature of the Son-Father relationship between Jesus and God (*e.g.* Mark 1:11; 9:7; 12:6; 13:32; 14:61–62; 15:39). Jesus directly addresses God as 'Father', with the very intimate Aramaic word 'Abba' being used (Mark 14:36). It is in John's gospel that the importance of the Father-Son relationship is brought out with especial clarity (*e.g.* John 5:16–27; 17:1–26). Here we find a remarkable emphasis upon the identity of will and purpose of the Father and Son, indicating how close is the relationship between Jesus and God. In the words of Jesus himself, as in the impression which was created among the first Christians, Jesus is clearly understood to have a unique and intimate relationship to God, which the resurrection demonstrated publicly (Romans 1:3–4).

Although all believers are sons of God in some sense of the word, Jesus is singled out as *the* Son of God. Paul distinguishes between Jesus as the *natural* Son of God, and believers as *adopted* sons (Romans 8:23; 9:4; Ephesians 1:5). Our relationship to God is quite different from Jesus' relationship to him, even though both may be referred to as 'sons of God'. Similarly, in 1 John, Jesus is referred to as the Son, while believers are designated as 'children'. There is something quite distinct about Jesus' relationship to God, as expressed in the title 'Son of God'.

For the Creed, stating that Jesus is the 'Son of God' amounts to saying that Jesus *is* God. We shall explore why this is the case later in this book. It is this belief which is often referred to as 'the incarnation' – in other words, that God became man in Jesus Christ (John 1:14). But why is this belief important? Two examples will illustrate why.

It is central to the gospel that we are saved through Jesus Christ: 'Salvation is found in no-one else' (Acts 4:12). You may know that a fish came to be a symbol of faith to the early Christians, because the five Greek letters spelling out 'fish' in Greek came to represent the slogan 'Jesus Christ, Son of God, Saviour.' For the New Testament, Jesus saves his people from their sins (Matthew 1:21); he is the Saviour born in Bethlehem (Luke 2:11); in his name alone is there salvation (Acts 4:12). Yet the Old Testament insists that it is God, and God alone, who can save and redeem his people (*e.g.* Isaiah 45:21–22). Unless Jesus is God, it is impossible for Jesus to save us.

Again, it is obvious that the first Christians worshipped and adored Jesus Christ – a practice which continues today. Thus 1 Corinthians 1:2 refers to

Christians as those who 'call upon the name of our Lord Jesus Christ', using language which reflects the Old Testament formulas for worshipping or adoring God himself (*e.g.* Genesis 4:26; 13:4; Psalm 105:1; Jeremiah 10:25; Joel 2:32). Yet, as every reader of the Old Testament knows, it is God *and God alone* who is to be worshipped (Exodus 20:3–7). And, as Paul reminded the Christians at Rome, there was a constant danger that people might worship creatures, when they ought to be worshipping their Creator instead (Romans 1:23). If Jesus was just another human being, a creature like the rest of us, the New Testament writers would be guilty of worshipping a creature! The insight that Jesus is the Son of God, however, disposes of this difficulty. Jesus *ought* to be worshipped and adored – precisely because he *is* God.

The ideas applied

Suppose we wanted to think about the love of God. We could say that it is infinite, boundless, beyond human telling, and so on. But all that we would have done is to speak of it abstractly and negatively, explaining what it is not. In fact, we are more or less saying that, whatever the love of God may be like, we can't say anything much about it. But the love of God is a rather important and exciting aspect of Christianity, something which we would clearly like to be able to talk about! Surely we can say something clear, intelligible, positive and exciting about it.

The basic problem here is that the human mind needs to think visually. It needs to picture God somehow. A picture, as we are often told, is worth a thousand words. Yet what pictures can we use?

There is every danger that we will choose something unreliable. But recognizing that Jesus is the Son of God, we can use Jesus himself as a picture of God. We can make a very positive and powerful statement about the love of God for man. The love of God is like the love of a man who lays down his life for his friends (John 15:13). Immediately, we are given a picture, an image, drawn from human experience. Here is something we can visualize and relate to. In the familiar and moving picture of Jesus laying down his life, giving his very being, for someone he loves, we have a most powerful, striking and moving statement of the full extent of the love of God for us. We can talk about the love of God in terms of our own experience, and supremely in terms of the tender image of Jesus Christ trudging to Calvary to die for those he loved. It is a moving, poignant and deeply evocative image, which we can easily imagine and identify with – in short, it is a statement about the love of God which speaks to us, which appeals to us, and which brings home exactly what the love of God is like. No longer need we be at a loss for words when we try to speak about the love of God to our friends, or picture it for ourselves.

Key scriptural passages

Mark 1:1–8; 2:1–13; John 1:14; 5:16–27; 17:1–26; Romans 1:3–4.

Questions for discussion

Why is it inadequate to describe Jesus just as a good religious teacher?

'Who can forgive sins but God alone?' Do you agree? And what are the implications for our understanding of who Jesus is? (Read Mark 2:1–13.)

In what ways does Jesus help us understand what God is like?

For further reading

F. F. Bruce, *The Real Jesus*. An excellent study of the identity and significance of Jesus for Christians.

R. T. France, *The Evidence for Jesus*. Excellent presentation of the historical evidence for Jesus.

Alister McGrath, *Understanding Jesus*. A lucid and easy-to-read guide to the main Christian beliefs about Jesus.

CHAPTER FIVE

Our Lord

HAVING already defined him as the 'Son of God', the Creed continues its description of Jesus Christ by referring to him as 'our Lord'.

The idea explained

'Let all Israel be assured of this; God has made this Jesus, whom you crucified, both Lord and Christ' (Acts 2:36). With these words, Peter echoes the common teaching of the New Testament – through the resurrection of Jesus, God has established his credentials as both Messiah and the Lord. We have already looked at the implications of the term 'Messiah' or 'Christ': the term 'Lord' now needs unpacking.

It is difficult to open the Old Testament without coming across the word 'Lord'. It is used, time and time again, to refer to God (*e.g.* Genesis 12:1; 15:6; 17:1; 39:2; Exodus 3:2). It is interesting to note that the Old Testament writers were reluctant to refer to God directly. God's name was regarded as too holy to be bandied about. When it was necessary to make reference to God, they generally used a 'cypher' of four letters YHWH (often referred to as the 'Tetragrammaton'). This group of letters, which lies behind the English Authorized Version's references to God as 'Jehovah', and the Jerusalem Bible's rather cryptic references to God as 'Yahweh', was used to represent the sacred name of God. When the Old Testament scriptures were translated from Hebrew into Greek, the Greek word *kyrios* – 'the Lord' – was used to translate the sacred name of God. Thus Josephus tells us that the Jews refused to call the Roman Emperor *kyrios*, because they regarded this name as reserved for God alone. Long before the New Testament period, the word 'Lord' thus came to refer to God himself.

The word 'Lord' is used in this same way in the New Testament. Jesus refers to God as 'the Lord' on several occasions (*e.g.* Matthew 4:10; 22:37). But an astonishing new development has taken place: it is now *Jesus* who is regularly referred to as 'the Lord' (*e.g.* Philippians 2:11; 3:8; Colossians 2:6). A word which was once used to refer to God has now come to refer to Jesus. Sometimes the word is used as little more than a polite title of respect. Thus when Martha speaks to Jesus, and addresses him as 'Lord' (John 11:21), she is probably – although not necessarily – merely treating Jesus with due respect. This, however, accounts only for a small number of the occurences of the word. The vast majority of them refer to Jesus as 'the Lord'. It is obvious that something of vital importance about Jesus' status is being said. But what? And why?

The confession that 'Jesus is Lord' (Romans 10:9; 1 Corinthians 12:3) was clearly regarded by Paul as a superb summary of the gospel. Christians are those who 'call upon the name of the Lord' (Romans 10:13; 1 Corinthians 1:2). They are those who have 'received Christ Jesus as Lord' (Colossians 2:6). Through the resurrection, God has established Jesus Christ as Lord, and publicly declared this to all of humanity (*e.g.* Acts 2:36). 'Jesus is Lord' means 'Jesus has been given the same status as God himself.' It is an affirmation that Jesus has the right to lordship over us, just as God has.

This point is made especially clear at several points in the New Testament at which an Old Testament reference to 'the Lord' (in other words, God) becomes a reference to 'the Lord Jesus'. Two examples are particularly interesting.

1. Acts 2:21. In his great sermon on the day of Pentecost (Acts 2:14–39), Peter quotes from the prophet Joel: 'everyone who calls on the name of the Lord will be saved' (Acts 2:21). It is obvious that Peter interprets this as a reference to Jesus Christ: God has made Jesus 'both Lord and Christ' (Acts 2:36), and anyone who repents and is baptized 'in the name of Jesus Christ' (Acts 2:38) will receive forgiveness of sins. Joel refers to a crucial period in the history of the people of God, in which the Spirit of God will be poured out upon all people (Joel 2:28). A 'great and dreadful day of the Lord' (that is, God: Joel 2:31) is foretold, on which the Spirit of the Lord will be poured out on the people of God; on that day, 'everyone who calls on the name of the Lord will be saved' (Joel 2:32) – in other words, everyone who calls upon the name of *God* will be saved. But for Peter, the 'Lord' in question is *Jesus*. Through his resurrection, Jesus has been declared to be the Lord. He now has the status and identity of God himself.

2. Philippians 2:10–11. In this famous passage, Paul declares that God has exalted Jesus, and that 'at the name of Jesus every knee should bow ... and every tongue confess that Jesus Christ is Lord'. Paul is here making use of Isaiah 45:23, in which God himself declares that one day every knee will bow before *him*, and every tongue confess *him*! In other words, Paul has felt it entirely appropriate, in the light of the resurrection, to take a great Old Testament prophecy referring to the Lord God, and apply it to the Lord Jesus.

Many other illustrations of this could be given – for example, Hebrews 1:10, which alters the reference of Psalm 102:25 from God to Jesus. This practice of transferring from one Lord (God) to another (Jesus) is known to have infuriated Jews at the time. Thus in the second-century dialogue between Trypho the Jew and Justin Martyr, Trypho complains that Christians have 'hijacked' passages referring to God, in order to refer them to Christ. There was, of course, no suggestion that there were two 'Lords' (in other words, two Gods) – simply that Jesus had to be regarded as having a status at least equal to that of God, which demanded that he be addressed and worshipped as God.

To believe that Jesus is Lord, therefore, involves more than believing that he has authority over us (although, as we shall see, that is certainly implied); it makes a direct and powerful claim about the divinity of Jesus Christ. To confess that Jesus Christ is Lord is to proclaim his equality with God. It makes a statement about Jesus' relation to *God*. It also, however, makes a statement about Jesus' relation to *us*. It affirms that he is, or should be, the Lord of our lives. It is at this point that the application of the Lordship of Jesus Christ becomes especially relevant.

The idea applied

Note that the Creed does not just refer to Jesus as *the* Lord; he is *our* Lord. Jesus Christ has a right to Lordship over our lives. This amounts to a demand for personal obedience and loyalty to Jesus Christ as our Lord and Saviour. If we do not recognize Jesus Christ as Lord, he is not *our* Lord, but someone else's. He has yet to be acknowledged as Lord of our lives. It is possible to pay lip-service to Jesus as Lord, yet deny him as Lord by the way in which we act (Matthew 7:21–22). To recognize that Jesus is Lord is to seek to do his will.

But Jesus Christ is not merely the Lord of our personal lives; he is also the Lord of the church. It is Jesus Christ which the church must obey. It is to Jesus Christ, and to no-one else, that the church owes her faithful obedience. Many Christians have been faced with a real dilemma over conflicts of loyalty. Often Jesus Christ seems to pull in one direction, and other influential and powerful individuals or bodies in another. Which is to be obeyed?

This was the choice faced by the German church in the 1930s, when Adolf Hitler came to power. He demanded that he and the government of the Third Reich should have authority over the church and its preaching. Alarmed by this development, representatives of the Protestant churches met at Barmen (29–31 May 1934). There they issued the famous *Barmen Declaration*, perhaps one of the finest statements of the Lordship of Jesus Christ over his church:

'I am the way, and the truth and the life. No-one comes to the Father except through me.' (John 14:6). 'I tell you the truth, the man who does not enter the sheep pen by the gate, but climbs in some other way, is a thief and a robber .... I am the gate; whoever enters through me will be saved' (John 10:1, 9).

Jesus Christ, as he is attested for us in Holy Scripture, is the one Word of God which we have to hear and which we have to trust and obey in life and in death. We reject the false doctrine, that the church could and would have to acknowledge as a source of her proclamation, apart from and besides this one Word of God, still other events and powers, figures and truths, as God's revelation.

In other words, the church cannot and must not substitute anything (for example, the state government) or anyone (such as Adolf Hitler) for Jesus Christ. If the church ever loses her faithful obedience to her Lord, she has lost her life and her soul.

At many points throughout the world the Christian church is under strain to conform to outside pressures. There is pressure for the church to conform to the values of secular liberal culture in the west. There is pressure for her to conform to the views of authoritarian regimes in southern Africa and South America. But if the Lordship of Christ is taken seriously, these pressures must be resisted. The church of Jesus Christ owes her loyalty, her existence and her future to the one who died in order that we might live – and God has declared *him* – and no-one and nothing else – as Lord of that church. A sobering thought, perhaps, but one which cannot be ignored.

Key scriptural passages

Matthew 7:21–22; Acts 2:14–39; Romans 10:9; 1 Corinthians 12:3; Philippians 2:5–11.

Questions for discussion

'Jesus is Lord!' Why is this an appropriate summary of the gospel?

Are there areas of your life from which Jesus Christ is excluded as Lord? Your career? Your business decisions? Your family life?

What pressures can you identify upon individual believers and churches to conform to others?

For further reading

F. F. Bruce, *The Real Jesus*. An excellent study of the identity and significance of Jesus for Christians.
R. T. France, *The Evidence for Jesus*. Excellent presentation of the historical evidence for Jesus.
Alister McGrath, *Understanding Jesus*. A lucid and easy-to-read guide to the main Christian beliefs about Jesus.

CHAPTER SIX

He was conceived by the power of the Holy Spirit, and born of the Virgin Mary

THE Creed now changes pace slightly. Having told us what to believe about Jesus, it begins to explore the foundations of those beliefs. An appeal is made to history – to the great acts by which the Christian faith was brought into being. The Creed rapidly takes us through the events of Christmas, Holy Week, Good Friday and Easter Day, as it unfolds the historical events on which the gospel is firmly based. First to be noted are the circumstances of the birth of Jesus.

The ideas explained

This section of the Creed takes up the key elements of two well-known scriptural passages, Matthew 1:18–25 and Luke 1:26–38. There are two components to this familiar statement of Christian belief. On the one hand, Jesus was born of a human mother (Galatians 4:4). He is a human being, like us. He was born into the world, like us; later, he would suffer and die, as we must one day suffer and die. Jesus really was a human being, with whom we can identify. But on the other hand, he was conceived by the Holy Spirit. From the moment of his conception, Jesus was marked out as unique. He is the 'Son of God' in every sense of the word. He did not become the Son of God at some point during his career; from the very beginning, he possessed exactly this status and identity. The way in which Jesus was conceived confirms what the crucifixion and resurrection declare – that Jesus is indeed both God and man.

Jesus was both God and man; really divine and really human at one and the same time. This was the conclusion forced on Christians as they reflected on the remarkable story of Jesus. Everything pointed to it. It was a very significant conclusion to draw – yet the first Christians felt the evidence compelled them to draw it. A number of alternative explanations of Jesus' identity and significance were given careful consideration, and rejected. Two are of particular importance.

1. Jesus was a man who God adopted as his Son; up to that point he was just an ordinary human being, like anyone else. Supporters of this theory (known as 'Adoptianism') suggested that the moment of Jesus' adoption was at his baptism. For these individuals, the words 'You are my Son, whom I love' (Mark 1:11) thus represented the moment of his adoption as the Son of God. The critics of this theory drew attention to scriptural passages stressing that Jesus was the Son of God from eternity (*e.g.* Colossians 1:15–23; Hebrews 1).

2. Jesus was a divine being who masqueraded as a human being. He just seemed to be human; in reality, he was nothing of the kind. His humanity was just an outward appearance, masking the fact

that Jesus was a totally divine being. This theory, known as 'Docetism' (from the Greek word meaning 'to appear or seem') was rejected as inconsistent with the many biblical texts which pointed to Jesus' humanity. Jesus hungered (Matthew 4:2), suffered (Luke 22:44), wept (John 11:33–35), was thirsty (John 19:28), and had real blood running through his veins (John 19:34). He really was a human being, like us – he *had* to be, if he was to save us. The mystery of the incarnation does not involve *denying* Jesus' humanity, but in recognizing that he was *at the same time* divine (John 1:14; 2 Corinthians 8:9; Philippians 2:5–11).

Note the explicit reference in the Creed to the virgin birth. This belief is of importance, for three reasons. First, it makes important connections with Old Testament prophecy (Isaiah 7:14; Matthew 1:22–23). Here, as elsewhere in his career, Jesus brings to fulfilment great Old Testament hopes (*cf.* Matthew 2:5–6, 14–15, 17–18). Second, it stresses that Jesus was divine by nature, not by adoption at a later date. Third, it provided an important defence against early Jewish opponents of Christianity, who suggested that Jesus was the illegitimate child of Mary (it is possible that this may be hinted at in John 8:41). It was often suggested by such hostile critics that Jesus was the illegitimate son of a Roman soldier – thus adding the suggestion of collaboration with the foreign army of occupation. It was a neat move, shrewdly designed to discredit Jesus in the eyes of his own people. The New Testament, however, has a rather different – and much more exciting – understanding of who the real father of Jesus was!

Why is it important to insist that Jesus is both God

and man, both divine and human? For a start, the evidence demands that conclusion. Christians believe it because it is the only interpretation of Jesus which does justice to him. But it is of vital importance in other respects. If Jesus Christ was not both divine and human, our redemption would be a virtual impossibility. Let us explore this briefly.

Christians believe that we are saved only through Jesus Christ. What does this actually imply? It is obvious that Jesus is a man, a human being like all of us. But if he is *just* a man, like the rest of us, he shares our need for redemption – in other words, he can't redeem us. He is part of our problem, not the solution to it. So there must be some essential difference between Jesus and man if Jesus is indeed to be our redeemer. After all, Christianity has always insisted that Jesus is the solution to our problem, rather than part of that problem! But if Jesus is God, and God alone, he has no point of contact with us. He cannot relate to those who need redemption. His humanity provides that point of contact. And so we arrive at the conclusion that Jesus must be divine and human if he is to redeem us.

We could develop the same idea along different lines. Imagine two people – let us call them 'A' and 'B' – who enjoy a close relationship, which breaks down completely over some misunderstanding. A is convinced that it is the fault of B, and B is sure that A is in the wrong. So strongly do they hold their views that they refuse to speak to each other. The situation is, unfortunately, all too familiar from everyday experience – whether it is a matter of personal relationships, or industrial or international relations. We all know situations where this has happened, and may even have been unfortunate enough to have been involved with them ourselves. But how can the situation be resolved? How can A and B become reconciled? It is clear that the situation demands a *mediator*, a *go-between*. But who is qualified to act in this capacity?

It will be obvious that the best mediator or go-between is someone who both A and B know and respect, but who will be impartial. Let us call this mediator 'C'. C must represent A to B, and B to A. He or she must not be identified with either A or B – yet must have points of contact with both if he or she is to be accepted. He or she must be close enough to both of them to represent them both, and yet sufficiently different from them both to prevent him or her being identified with either.

The idea of Jesus being the one and only go-between or mediator between God and sinful humanity is deeply ingrained in the New Testament. 'For there is one God, and one mediator between God and men, the man Christ Jesus' (1 Timothy 2:5). Paul talks about God 'reconciling' us to himself through Jesus Christ (2 Corinthians 5:18–19). What is particularly interesting is that Paul uses the same Greek word to refer to the restoration of the relationship between God and humanity which he had used earlier to refer to the restoration of a broken relationship between a man and his wife (1 Corinthians 7:10–11). Christ is understood to act as the mediator or go-between, in restoring the relation between God and humanity to what it once was. And now we can start applying the ideas we discussed in the previous paragraph. This mediator must represent God to man, and man to God. He must have points of contact with both God and man, and yet be distinguishable from them both. And so on. In short, the central Christian idea of the incarnation, which expresses the belief that Jesus is both God and man, divine and human, portrays Jesus as the perfect mediator between God and man. He, and he alone is able to redeem us and reconcile us to God.

The ideas applied

Many of us feel low at points. We find resisting temptation difficult. We are frightened by the thought of suffering and death. It is here that the doctrine of the incarnation has a vital contribution to make. Through Christ, God knows what it is like to be tempted. He knows what it is like to suffer. When we pray in such situations, we don't have to *explain* to God what it is like – he already knows. He has been through it himself. He has experienced it at first hand. This is a deeply consoling thought: we have a God who knows and understands our weaknesses. He is someone who we can approach in trust.

Suppose someone comes to you, and explains that he is going through a difficult patch. His mother died recently, and he feels totally lost. Naturally, you want to help. Your own mother is still alive, however. So you try to think what it must be like to lose your mother. You try to think yourself into his situation. You imagine what he is going through, and try to respond accordingly. That is *empathy*, a very useful tool for counselling individuals. But now try and imagine a different situation. Your own mother died recently. Immediately, you can relate to this man. You have shared a common experience. 'I know just how you must feel!', you can reply. Can you see how much more credible and helpful that makes you to this man? Can you understand how he will find you easy to talk to as a result? He will feel that you understand him. That is *sympathy* – where your care is based on a shared experience. When you are tempted or suffer, remember that God sympathizes with you. God has no need to empathize with you. He has been through it before you (Hebrews 4:14–16). Take comfort from that thought.

Key scriptural passages

Matthew 1:18–25; Luke 1:26–38; Philippians 2:5–11; Hebrews 4:14–16.

Questions for discussion

How would you explain the significance of Christmas to an interested inquirer?

'God with us.' How helpful is this as a way of thinking about the incarnation?

Look at the words of some well-known Christmas carols (such as *Hark the herald angels sing!*, *In the bleak midwinter*, and *O come all ye faithful*). How do they express the Christmas gospel? What themes do they identify as important?

For further reading

Norman Anderson, *The Mystery of the Incarnation*. A helpful account of many of the ideas discussed in this chapter.

Alister McGrath, *Understanding Jesus*, pp. 91–119. A clear discussion of what it means to speak of Jesus being both God and man, and why this is of such importance to the gospel.

Jonathan Webster, *God is here!* A useful and readable introduction to many of the themes of the incarnation.

CHAPTER SEVEN

He suffered under Pontius Pilate

THIS article, and that which immediately follows, develop the theme of the humanity of Christ. The Creed recounts a series of events which firmly establish that Jesus Christ was a real human being of flesh and blood – like us.

The ideas explained

Some Christians find it surprising that Pontius Pilate should be mentioned in the Creed. A few even find it offensive. Nevertheless, the governor (or procurator) of Judaea from AD 26 – 36 has found his way into the Creed. And it is very important that he should be there! The fifth-century writer Rufinus wrote as follows: 'Those who handed down the Creed showed great wisdom in emphasizing the actual date at which these things happened, so that there might be no chance of any uncertainty or vagueness upsetting the stability of the tradition.' The reference to Pilate firmly anchors the Creed to history. It affirms that we are dealing with an event – the crucifixion of Jesus Christ – which actually happened in history. The gospel is not like some fairy tale, which happened 'long, long, ago and far, far, away' – its central event happened in a definite place and at a definite time (Luke 3:1–3).

Why is it so important to emphasize this point? Because you and I both live in history. The gospel affirms that God himself entered into that history, in order to meet us and redeem us. God came down to meet us where we are, in time and space. The doctrine of the incarnation tells us that God came down to our level, in order to bring us up to his. There is a certain down-to-earth realism about the Christian faith. And this is partly grounded in the fact that God came down to our earth from heaven to meet us, and bring us home. The gospel is not just about *ideas* – it is about God *acting, and continuing to act, in history*.

Mention of Pilate also brings out the public nature of Jesus' trial, suffering and crucifixion. Pilate here represents the witness of the world to the suffering and death of its unacknowledged Saviour. The final days of Jesus' ministry took place in full public view, where all could see what was happening. The crucifixion, for example, took place in public, under the gaze of the citizens of Jerusalem. It was thus impossible for anyone to deny that these things had happened.

Pilate is also of importance in another respect. Within the Creed, Pilate represents the rejection of Jesus Christ by his world – a major theme of the New Testament. The disowning of Jesus is seen as representing the rejection of the Creator by his creation. The New Testament portrays that rejection in many ways: Jesus is rejected by those who had known him from his youth at Nazareth (Luke 4:16–30). He was condemned as a blasphemer by the leaders of the Jewish people (Matthew 26:59–66). He was condemned as a political threat to the stabilty of the *pax Romana* in the region by Pilate.

It would be wrong to isolate any of these groups, and place the burden of Jesus' crucifixion upon them, and them alone. For the New Testament, the behaviour of the synagogue congregation at Nazareth, the Jewish leaders and the Roman procurator all point to the same thing – the sinfulness of human nature. All human beings, no matter who they are or when they live, are sinners, needing God's forgiveness and reconciliation. It is sinful human nature itself which led the creation to crucify its Creator. Sin bites so deep into human nature that it comes close to destroying our ability to recognize God when he comes amongst us.

So deep-rooted is sin that we are incapable of breaking its strangle-hold unaided. It enslaves us. It is like an addictive drug, which destroys the will and the ability of individuals to break free from its grip. The gospel affirms that God has acted to break the hold of sin upon us. Through the death of Jesus Christ, God is able to transform our situation. The guilt of sin is forgiven; its power is broken; its stain is cleansed. But the Creed asks us to consider the cost of this breakthrough. Forgiveness is a costly business, which demanded the suffering and death of the Son of God. Jesus Christ really suffered in order that our real sins might really be forgiven.

The close relation between suffering and redemption is clearly brought out in Isaiah 52:13 – 53:12. This powerful and moving passage describes a mysterious suffering servant. He was innocent; he suffered on behalf of the guilty. Through his sufferings, others will be healed.

> He was despised and rejected by men, a man of sorrows, and familiar with suffering .... Surely he took up our infirmities and carried our sorrows, yet we considered him stricken by God, smitten by him, and afflicted. But he was pierced for our transgressions, he was crushed for our iniquities; the punishment that brought us peace was upon him, and by his wounds we are healed. We all, like sheep, have gone astray, each of us has turned to his own way; and the Lord has laid on him the iniquity of us all .... For he bore the sin of many, and made intercession for the transgressors.

The New Testament writers saw this passage fulfilled in the suffering of Jesus Christ (*e.g.* see 1 Peter 3:21–25). His sufferings on the cross were not pointless or accidental, but the mysterious and wonderful way in which God was working out the salvation of the world.

The sufferings of Jesus also have a direct bearing on the mystery of human suffering in general. The twentieth century has witnessed previously unimagined horrors of human suffering in the trenches of the First World War, in the extermination camps of Nazi Germany, and the programmes of genocide established by Nazi Germany and Marxist Cambodia. A movement known as 'Protest Atheism' grew up in response to these developments. 'We cannot believe in a God who stays safely in his heaven,' it declared, 'while all this suffering goes on. We cannot take that sort of God seriously. If he doesn't know what it is like to suffer, he cannot know anything about us.' But, as we have seen, the gospel declares that God does indeed know what it is like to suffer. He is not uninvolved with its pain and misery. It is certainly true that any view of God which denies the incarnation, and speaks of God being far-off and distant, is very vulnerable to the charges of Protest Atheism – a point which reminds us of how important and relevant the doctrine of the incarnation is. The Creed, however, as we have seen, knows of God subjecting himself to the evil and pain of the world at its worst, in the grim scene at Calvary, bearing the brunt of that agony itself. God suffered in Christ, taking upon himself the suffering and pain of the world which he created.

The ideas applied

Suffering is a mystery which causes anguish to many Christians. It seems to call the love of God into question. The suffering of Jesus Christ upon the cross at Calvary does not explain suffering. It does, however, reveal that God himself is willing and able to allow himself to be subject to all the pain and suffering which his creation experiences. We are not talking of a God who stands far off from his world, aloof and distant from its problems. We are dealing with a loving God who has entered into our human situation, who became man and dwelt among us as one of us. We know a God who, in his love for us, determined to experience at first hand what it is like to be frail, mortal and human, to suffer and to die. We cannot explain suffering, but we can say that, in the person of his Son Jesus Christ, God took it upon himself to follow this way. God became the man of suffering, so that we can enter into the mystery of death and resurrection. God knows what it is like to be human – an astonishing and comforting thought. God is not like a general who issues orders to his troops from the safety of a bomb-proof shelter, miles away from the front line, but one who leads his troops from the front, having previously done all that he asks them to do in turn. If God asks us to suffer on his behalf, it is because he has already suffered on our behalf.

The suffering and pain of the world simply will not go away, and we have every right to dismiss those who tell us that one day all will be well – after we have adopted their particular solution to the world's ills. Realism now demands that we work towards the alleviation of misery and suffering, recognizing that the vision of its total elimination is Utopian. The idea of a political revolution which will eliminate human misery and suffering has lost what little credibility it once had, and has probably caused just as much misery where this hypothesis has become a dogma. Now that Marxism has lost its hold on the countries of Eastern Europe, for example, its total failure to change the human predicament – despite all its promises – has become increasingly obvious.

What, then, may one say about God and suffering? Can anything be said which is of comfort? In the history of the world, four answers have been given. First, suffering is real, and will not go away. But death comes as the end, and in death there is an end of suffering, and eventual peace. Second, suffering is an illusion. It simply is not there, but is imagined. Third, suffering is real – but we ought to be able to rise above it, and recognize that it is of little importance. The Christian has the fourth answer: God suffered in Christ. God knows what it is like to suffer. The letter to the Hebrews talks about Jesus being our 'sympathetic High Priest' (Hebrews 4:15) – someone who suffers along with us (which is the literal meaning of both the Greek word *sympathetic* and the Latin word *compassionate*). This thought does not explain suffering, although it may make it more tolerable to bear. For it is expressing the deep insight that God himself suffered at first hand as we suffer. We are given a new perspective on life. Christianity has always held that it is the suffering of Christ upon the cross which is the culmination and fulfilment of his ministry. God shares in the darkest moments of his people. God can be found in suffering. There is a famous saying about the medical profession worth remembering here: 'Only the wounded physician can heal.' The God who offers to heal the wounds of our sin has himself been wounded by sinners.

Key scriptural passages

Isaiah 52:13 – 53:12; Matthew 27:11–56; John 19:1–16.

Questions for discussion

Does suffering help us to grow in our faith?

In what ways do the following Old Testament passages help us gain a deeper understanding of the sufferings of Jesus: Psalm 22; Isaiah 52:13 – 53:12. (You may find it helpful to follow through the New Testament use of these passages, using marginal references).

In what ways are the things you suffer related to your faith? (1 Peter 4:12–19 is important in this respect).

For further reading

Peter Kreeft, *Making Sense out of Suffering.* Full of insights and helpful thoughts on the mystery of suffering.

C. S. Lewis, *The Problem of Pain.* A characteristically lucid discussion.

Warren Wiersbe, *Why Us?* A valuable popular guide to some of the questions raised by human suffering.

CHAPTER EIGHT

He was crucified, died and buried. He descended to the dead

THIS section of the Creed calls to mind the scene at Calvary. It was perhaps the darkest moment the disciples had ever faced, as Jesus died on the first Good Friday.

The ideas explained

Jesus was crucified. The word 'crucified' would have sent a shudder down the spine of any educated person in the ancient world. It was familiar as a form of execution to east and west, to Roman and Greek, to Gentile and Jew. It was perhaps the most barbaric form of execution known, ideally suited as a deterrent. It seems to have been used especially by the Romans in the suppression of rebellious provincials, such as the Cantabrians in northern Spain and the Jews in Judaea. Josephus' accounts of the crucifixion of countless Jewish fugitives who attempted to escape from besieged Jerusalem make horrifying reading. In the view of most Roman jurists, notorious criminals should be crucified on the exact location of their crime, so that 'the sight may deter others from such crimes'. Perhaps for this reason, Quintillian crucified criminals on the busiest thoroughfares, in order that the maximum deterrent effect might be achieved.

In crucifixion, the sadism of the executioners was given full rein. It is difficult to give a desciption of what a 'normal' crucifixion would have looked like; however, there are ample descriptions of the practice dating from Roman times to allow us to build up a picture of the various possibilities open to Roman executioners. (It is, incidentally, interesting to notice that classical Roman writers are often reluctant to write in any detail on the subject, apparently on account of its gruesome nature. The Roman writer Seneca wrote briefly of his experience of crucifixions: 'I see crosses there, not just of one type, but made in different ways: some hang their victims head downwards, some impale their private parts, others stretch their arms out on them.') However, it is clear that the detailed accounts of Jesus' crucifixion given in the gospels agree well with contemporary Roman practice.

The victim would usually be flogged, and was often forced to carry the cross-beam to the place of execution. When this place was reached, the victim's arms were generally nailed to the cross-beam. This was then raised up. Far from being an essentially bloodless form of execution, as some commentators have suggested, the victim would have bled profusely. Only if he had not been flogged or tortured previously, and bound, rather than nailed, to the cross, would no blood have been spilled. But death was not usually due to loss of blood. The victim found it increasingly difficult to breathe, due to the strain placed on his chest by the sheer weight of his body. Eventually, he would die from exhaustion, unable to breathe. The Roman executioners often prolonged this agony by providing a small wooden seat (known as a *sedile*) on the main upright beam of the cross. The result was the same; it now took much longer. The gospel descriptions of Jesus' crucifixion agree well with our knowledge of traditional Roman practices. The gospels portray a man who is dying from lack of breath – who finally cries his memorable and moving last words (John 19:30), and then breathes no more.

Jesus, then, was given over to 'the utterly vile death of the cross' (to quote the words of Origen, an early Christian writer). To say that Jesus died, or just that he was executed, misses the full barbarism of the way in which he died. The full sadism of human nature was brought to bear on him. It was a shameful and degrading death. It is therefore small wonder that the pagan world of the first century reacted with disbelief or disgust to the Christians' suggestion that they should obey and worship 'an evil man and his cross' (to quote an early critic of Christianity). Crucifixion was a punishment reserved for the lowest criminals, clearly implying that Jesus was one of their number. Jesus 'endured the cross, scorning its shame' (Hebrews 12:2). It is small wonder that many regarded the Christian gospel as utter foolishness (1 Corinthians 1:23–25).

But the gospel is not merely about the fact that Jesus died, nor even that he was executed, nor yet that he was crucified. He died *for us*. Paul makes this point as follows: 'What I received I passed on to you as of first importance: that Christ died for our sins according to the Scriptures' (1 Corinthians 15:3). Christianity is not just about the historical fact that

Jesus was crucified; it is about the astonishing and thrilling truth that he died in order that we might be forgiven. Paul makes a clear distinction between the *event* of the death of Christ, and the *significance* of this event. That Christ died is a simple matter of history; that Christ died *for our sins* is the gospel itself.

The vital distinction between an event and its meaning can be brought out by considering an example. In 49 BC Julius Caesar crossed a small river with a single legion of men. The name of that river was the Rubicon, and it marked the boundary between Italy and Cisalpine Gaul. As an event, it was not particularly interesting; it was not a particularly wide river, and it had been crossed countless times before. But this seemingly unimportant event had a deeper meaning. The Rubicon marked a national frontier. By crossing it, Caesar declared war against Pompey and the Roman senate – with momentous results. The *event* was the crossing of a river; the *meaning* of that event was a declaration of war.

In many ways, the death of Christ may be said to parallel Caesar's crossing of the Rubicon. The event itself appears unexceptional, except to those who know its significance. Jesus died upon a cross. On the basis of contemporary records, we know that an incalculable number of people died in this way at that time. Lots of other people had died unjustly in history before then – think of Socrates, for example. Anyway, we all have to die at some point. As an event, it hardly seems important or noteworthy. On the other hand, those aware of the meaning of an event saw behind the mere external event itself, to what it signified, to the reason why it was important. Pompey and the Roman senate were not interested in the mechanics of how Caesar crossed the Rubicon – for them, it meant war. Paul was not particularly interested in the mechanics of the crucifixion of Jesus – for him, it meant salvation, forgiveness and victory over death. Thus the 'word of the cross' was not the proclamation of the simple fact that Jesus was crucified, but with the significance of this event for us.

Finally, we may pause to look at the final sentence in this section. 'He descended to the dead.' What does this mean? It is a statement of the belief that Jesus *really did die*. For the New Testament writers, Christ was not raised 'from death' (an abstract idea), but 'from the dead' (Acts 2:24; Romans 1:4; Colossians 2:12). The Greek term literally means 'out of those who are dead'. In other words, Jesus shared the fate of all those who have died. Again, we find the same point being stressed: Jesus really was human, like us. His divinity does not compromise his humanity in this respect. Being God incarnate did not mean he was spared from tasting death. He did not merely seem to die; he really did die, and joined those who had died before him. And in the glorious act of resurrection, God raised him from the dead – but that is to anticipate the subject of the next chapter!

The ideas applied

Many Christians find themselves confused and upset by not experiencing God as present and active in the world. If you feel this way, try to imagine what it was like for the disciples on the first Good Friday. They had given up everything to follow Jesus. Then, in front of their eyes, he was taken from them to be publicly executed. You can feel an immense sense of despair as you read the gospel accounts of the death of Jesus. Perhaps the disciples were hoping for a miracle. Yet there seemed to be no trace of God's presence or activity at Calvary. As Jesus became weaker, the disciples must have become increasingly despondent. There was no sign of God intervening to transform the situation.

Finally, Jesus died. That would probably have been the darkest moment in the lives of the disciples. They were already demoralized enough, as Peter's denial of Jesus demonstrated. Now, as they watched the scene from a distance, it must have seemed as if their entire world had collapsed, shown up as a fraud and an illusion.

Of course, we know the outcome of that story. We know how the disciples' sorrow was transformed to joy and wonder, as the news of the resurrection of Jesus became known. But try to imagine yourself standing among the disciples as they watched Jesus suffer and die – *without* knowing that he would be raised again from the dead. Set aside your knowledge of what happens later, and try to imagine what it must have been like to watch Jesus die on the cross. His suffering seemed utterly pointless. And where was God in all this? It was all enough to make anyone doubt whether God existed in the first place. It is easy to get a feel for the sense of despair and bewilderment on that sad day.

All those doubts were resolved through the resurrection. The apparently pointless suffering of Jesus was revealed as the means through which God was working out the salvation of sinful humanity. God was not absent from that scene; he was working to transform it from a scene of hopelessness and helplessness to one of joy and hope. God's love was *demonstrated*, not contradicted, by the death of his son (John 3:16; Romans 5:8).

So thinking about the first Good Friday brings home to us how unreliable experience and feelings can be as guides to the presence of God. Those around the cross didn't experience the presence of God – so they concluded that he was absent from the scene. The resurrection overturns that judgment: God was present in a hidden manner, which experience mistook for his absence. Do you feel that God is absent from your life, or from certain difficult situations? Are you bewildered by events, or in despair over the way things are going? Then think of the first Good Friday, when God also seemed to be absent, only to be shown to have been working in a hidden and mysterious way to transform it in a totally unexpected manner. The promise of resurrection was there (Matthew 20:17–19). Yet, in the desperation of that terrible moment, that promise had been forgotten, perhaps even doubted. Experience seemed to suggest it could not be fulfilled. The first Good Friday reminds us of the need to trust in the divine promises made to us, rather than rely on our feelings and experience. Our feelings are influenced by a huge variety of factors: our health, the weather, the state of our bank balance, our personal relationships, our work or career – just to name the more obvious ones! God doesn't cease to exist just because you've had a bad day at the office or had an argument with a friend. Trust in the promises of God – not your emotional state.

Key scriptural passages

Matthew 27:32–66; Luke 23:26–56; John 19:16–42.

Questions for discussion

Why were the first Christians regarded as 'foolish' by their critics?

If there was no resurrection, what would the meaning of the cross have been?

How does the cross help us put experience in its proper perspective?

For further reading

Martin Hengel, *Crucifixion*. Perhaps the most detailed study of the way in which crucifixion was used in the ancient world, and how it was regarded by people at the time.

Leon Morris, *The Apostolic Preaching of the Cross*. A fine study of the New Testament understanding of the significance of the cross.

John Stott, *The Cross of Christ*. Invaluable on the meaning of the cross for Christian doctrine and life.

CHAPTER NINE

On the third day he rose again

THE Creed now moves on to recount the momentous events of the first Easter Day, as we turn to consider the resurrection of Jesus from the dead.

The idea explained

The Creed asserts that Jesus really was raised on the third day. We have already seen that the Creed stresses that Jesus really did die. But what happened next? Of course, some critics of Christianity, in an attempt to discredit the resurrection accounts of the New Testament, have suggested that he merely fainted or swooned on the cross. When Jesus recovered, his disciples thought he had been raised from the dead. Here's the theory that H. E. G. Paulus put forward in 1828.

In first century Palestine, it was quite common for people to be buried when they weren't actually dead. And this is exactly what happened with Jesus. He fainted on the cross. Jesus' body was then taken to a grave. The smell of the spices in which he was wrapped, and the coolness of the tomb, combined to revive him. So, on the Sunday morning, he was able to leave the tomb. (Fortunately, the great stone which had blocked the entrance had been moved by an earthquake.) After that, Jesus put in the occasional appearance to his disciples. These disciples, of course, being unsophisticated and backward peasants, thought that he was risen from the dead.

Now it is possible that someone who is deliberately determined not to believe in the resurrection may find this a convincing explanation. Even many critics of Christianity, however, find it totally implausible, saying little for the credibility of those who suggest it. It is just not an adequate explanation. Is it really likely that experienced Roman executioners would have botched up Jesus' execution? It seems that an executioner who allowed his victim to survive would have been put to death in his place. Would such executioners have been likely to confuse fainting and dying? The reference to 'blood and water' when Jesus' side was pierced after the crucifixion (John 19:34) would seem to be a reference to separation of the blood into clot and serum, indicating that Jesus was unequivocally dead. As this seems not to have been known at the time when John's gospel was written, it is unlikely to have been included to make the account seem more plausible.

No fundamental criticism, no decisive argument, has yet to be made which obliges Christians to give up faith in the resurrection of Jesus. For everyone who tries to discredit the resurrection, others have arisen to defend it with equal force.

Why is the resurrection of Jesus so important? Basically, it is important because it gives us crucial insights about God, about Jesus – and about ourselves. Let us explore these three areas.

1. *It tells us about God.* Scripture often defines God in terms of what he does. Someone might ask, 'What God do you believe in?' Of course, one answer might be that there only is one God, and that is all that there is to it. But a more helpful answer to the question would go something like this. The God of Israel is the God who revealed himself to Abraham, Isaac and Jacob; the God who led the people of Israel out of Egypt and into the promised land with great signs and wonders. In other words, we tell a story about God, which helps us understand who he is. The Old Testament identifies God from the history of his people – the great stories of Abraham, Isaac and Jacob, of the Exodus from Egypt, and so on, are told, in order to identify God. Question: who is God? Answer: whoever got us out of Egypt! (*e.g.*Exodus 19:4–5; Deuteronomy 26:5–9; Ezekiel 20:5–26).

Now we turn to the God who Christians worship and adore. Who is this God? To answer this question, the New Testament tells a story – perhaps the most famous story in the world – the story of Jesus Christ. And as that story reaches its climax in the account of the resurrection of Jesus from the dead, we learn that God, for Christians, is the one who acted in this way to raise Jesus. Question: Who is the God who Christians worship and adore? Answer: Whoever 'raised Jesus our Lord from the dead' (Romans 4:24). Of course, the New Testament writers make it abundantly clear that the one who 'raised Jesus our Lord from the dead' is the same God who got Israel out of Egypt – but the New Testament emphasis falls upon the resurrection of Jesus. Christians believe in a living and active God – the God who raised Christ from the dead, and will one day do the same for us. He is a God who acts.

2. *It tells us about Jesus.* Jesus Christ 'was declared with power to be the Son of God by his resurrection from the dead' (Romans 1:4). The resurrection singles out Jesus as unique. It demonstrates his vital unity with God himself. The central and decisive Christian doctrine of the divinity of Jesus Christ is grounded in his resurrection from the dead. The resurrection answers the question, 'Who is it who died upon the cross of Calvary?' It declares that the Jesus who died upon the cross is none other than the Son of God. Jesus is not merely another human being suffering unjust and cruel execution at the hands of an oppressive government; he is the Son of God, suffering pain and rejection *for us*.

For Paul, the cross reveals the tender love of God for sinners, such as himself (Romans 5:8; Galatians 2:20). This crucial insight, however, depends on recognizing that it is indeed the Son of God who died upon the cross. Without this truth – grounded and revealed in the resurrection of Jesus – the cross loses its saving significance. For if it is not God who is dying upon the cross, then it is not the love of God which is demonstrated. It is the love of a man for his fellow human beings – an especially splendid man, who may be ranked with others in history who have made equally great sacrifices for those who they loved. But the gospel is not about the love of one human being for another – it is about the love of God for us, which stimulates a new love of human beings for one another (1 John 4:10–11). To lose sight of the divinity of Christ is to lose for ever the insight that it is God himself who shows his love for us on the cross. What the cross might conceivably demonstrate is the full extent of the love of one human being for others. C. S. Lewis wrote on this matter to his friend Arthur Greaves on 11 December 1944: 'The doctrine of Christ's divinity seems to me not something stuck on which you can unstick but something that peeps out at every point so that you'd have to unravel the whole web to get rid of it.' The case of the love of God revealed in the death of Jesus Christ (John 3:16) is a case in point.

3. *It tells us about ourselves as believers.* The New Testament makes it clear that believers share in the fate of their Lord (Romans 6:1–10). Faith binds us to Jesus Christ, so that we share in his inheritance. Through adoption, we are the children of God, and entitled to the same riches which Christ gained. And that includes resurrection and glorification. Christ is the 'firstfruits' of the resurrection harvest (1 Corinthians 15:20); we shall follow in due course. Those who, through faith, are united to Jesus Christ will one day share in his resurrection. What our Lord is, we shall be as well.

But this must not be regarded as triumphalism. It is not 'pie in the sky when you die'. The New Testament reminds us that our place is firmly on this earth. There is no place for a faith that is so heavenly-minded that it is no earthly use. There is no resurrection without suffering and the cross. Just as Jesus suffered rejection, pain and death before he was raised, so we must expect to share his sufferings (1 Peter is an especially fine discussion of this theme). There is no cheap grace, no economy road to salvation. No cross, no resurrection. 'We share in his sufferings in order that we may also share in his glory' (Romans 8:17). God's gift of Christ-like glorification is given along with the gift of Christ-like suffering.

The idea applied

Many people are terrified of the idea of death. The fact that they will one day cease to exist frightens them. One way of dealing with this is to deny death. In his famous book *The Denial of Death*, Ernest Becker pointed out how many humans spent the best part of their lives trying to deny that they were going to die. 'Death is something that happens to someone else. It won't happen to me!' And so such people build their lives on a grand illusion. In reality, they are frightened and anxious – but they project the appearance of success, permanence and calm. Some Christians are also anxious about death, and wonder what to make of it.

It is here that the gospel has enormous implications. Jesus Christ suffered and died 'so that by his death he might destroy him who holds the power of death – that is, the devil – and free those who all their lives were held in slavery by their fear of death' (Hebrews 2:14–15). We are not talking about some soothing words to ease the pain of death and dying, which have no foundation in reality – such as saying 'It's all right', when in reality things could not be worse. No! We are talking about a *real* and *decisive* victory over death, by which its power is broken. A new attitude to death and dying is possible, because a new situation has dawned. Through faith, we are given the privilege of sharing in the resurrection of Jesus Christ. 'Thanks be to God! He gives us the victory through our Lord Jesus Christ' (1 Corinthians 15:57). 'Praise be to the God and Father of our Lord Jesus Christ! In his great mercy he has given us new birth into a living hope through the resurrection of Jesus Christ from the dead, and into an inheritance that can never perish, spoil or fade' (1 Peter 1:3–4). Socrates may have taught us how to die with dignity – but after Jesus Christ, human beings are able to suffer and die in real hope. Try and make that hope a visible part of your life, and explain it to your friends (1 Peter 3:15). For as long as human beings must die, the gospel has vital and relevant things to say! Make sure it gets a hearing in your circle of friends.

Key scriptural passages

Matthew 28:1–20; John 20:1–23; 1 Corinthians 15:1–28.

Questions for discussion

What is the difference between the resurrection of Lazarus (John 11) and the resurrection of Jesus?

If Jesus is not raised from the dead, why are we 'to be pitied more than all men' (1 Corinthians 15:19)?

Why is the resurrection so important for St Paul?

For further reading

Michael Green, *The Empty Cross of Jesus*. A splendid account of the meaning of the cross and the evidence for the resurrection, and its relevance for us today.

Michael Green, *The Day Death Died*. A very readable introduction to the resurrection – highly recommended.

Alister McGrath, *Understanding Jesus*, pp. 63–80. A concise summary of the main lines of evidence for the resurrection.

CHAPTER TEN

He ascended into heaven, and is seated at the right hand of the Father

THE Creed now moves forward from Easter Day to Ascension Day. This took place forty days after the resurrection (Acts 1:3), and it is thus celebrated on the sixth Thursday after Easter Day.

The ideas explained

The basic ideas stated in this section of the Creed can be summed up thus: Jesus was 'exalted to the right hand of God' (Acts 2:33). In the resurrection, Jesus was liberated from the bonds of death; now he is restored to the close presence, power and majesty of his Father. The story of the ascension is only related in Acts 1:1–11; however, the basic idea which it expresses may be found throughout the New Testament. Jesus is the 'great high priest who has gone through the heavens' (Hebrews 4:14; 9:11–12). Jesus, having come down to earth from heaven to redeem us, now returns to heaven to intercede for us. He came down to earth from heaven in great humility; he returned to heaven in triumph and glory, having accomplished all that was necessary for our salvation. 'God exalted him to the highest place and gave him the name that is above every name' (Philippians 2:9).

But notice the effect of the ascension on the disciples. They don't remain standing, rooted to the spot, completely overwhelmed by the fact that Jesus has returned to heaven. Their thoughts return immediately to earth – for there is work to be done. The ascended Christ commissions them to carry on his work on earth. 'All authority in heaven and on earth has been given to me. Therefore go and make disciples of all nations' (Matthew 28:18–19). In his Acts of the Apostles, Luke tells us that the disciples left the mountain of the ascension, and plunged themselves headlong into the needs of the world for which Christ died. They preached and healed; they proclaimed the good news to all by word and deed. Faith in the ascension does not mean any diminished interest in the world – it means a renewed commitment to that world, and new resources with which to meet its needs and cares.

In no way does the ascension of Christ mean that Christ is now *absent* from his world. It is utterly impossible to read Acts, and gain the impression that Jesus is no longer present with his people! The ascension does not mean, and was never intended to mean, that Christ is now restricted to some very limited region! Far from it. Through the resurrection, Christ broke down the barriers of time and space, allowing himself to be available to all (symbolized by the ripping of the temple curtain, Matthew 27:51). The doctrine of the ascension assures us that Christ has been exalted and glorified and that his power and glory can be revealed and reflected in our lives. The ascended Christ lives in believers through the Spirit (Galatians 2:20). The Christ who was exalted to heaven may also be exalted in our lives (Philippians 1:20). He is able to knock at the door of our lives (Revelation 3:20–21). We must not allow the limitations of our reason and imaginations to impose restrictions on what the risen and exalted Christ can do!

Finally, the Creed states that Jesus now sits at the right hand of God (Colossians 3:1). This is a very powerful image. Two main ideas are suggested, each of considerable importance.

1. *It suggests special favour and status.* To be allowed to sit at the right hand of a dignitary is a special favour (Psalm 16:8; 110:1). Not even the angels are allowed to sit at God's right hand (Hebrews 1:13). Jesus being allocated this place of honour thus confirms his unique status. It confirms all that we said earlier concerning Jesus' unique status and relationship to God. Jesus is enthroned beside the Father, crowned with glory and honour (Hebrews 2:7–9) on account of the great victory he gained over sin and death, through obedience to his Father's will. The mocking crown of thorns has now been replaced with a glorious crown of gold. This is the scene captured in the vision of John: 'Worthy is the Lamb, who was slain, to receive power and wealth and wisdom and strength and honour and glory and praise!' (Revelation 5:12).

2. *It suggests that Jesus has the Father's ear.* The New Testament insists that the risen, ascended and glorified Christ intercedes for us (Romans 8:34; Hebrews 7:25). Sitting at God's right hand, Jesus is able to plead our case for us. Christians pray in the name of Jesus Christ, acknowledging that the effectiveness

of their prayers rests upon what Jesus Christ has achieved in the past, and will achieve in the future. This point is made well in Charles Wesley's famous ascension hymn, *Hail the day that sees him rise*:

Still for us he intercedes, Alleluia!
His prevailing death he pleads, Alleluia!
Near himself prepares our place, Alleluia!
He the first-fruits of our race, Alleluia!

The ideas applied

Frederick Langbridge once penned the following lines:

Two men look out through the same bars:
One sees the mud, and one the stars..

It is quite possible for two people to be in exactly the same situation, and yet see it in quite different ways. Two men, looking out through the same prison bars, see very different things. One looks down, and sees the mud; the other lifts his eyes to heaven, and sees the stars. The point that Langbridge is trying to make is that some people see nothing but the rut of everyday life, ending in death, while others raise their eyes to heaven, knowing that their ultimate destiny lies with God. Their situation is more or less the same – but their outlooks are totally different.

One of the main differences between a believer and a non-believer is their attitudes to life. The non-believer often adopts an 'eat, drink and be merry, for tomorrow we die' attitude (1 Corinthians 15:32). If there is nothing more to life than this earth, we might as well enjoy it while we can. Let's not even think about death; let's deny that it will ever happen to *us*. Perhaps you know people in this situation. Their lives are not just firmly rooted in this world; they are trapped by it. They pursue 'happiness' and the pleasures of this world, thinking that they are conquering the world – when in fact they are conquered by it.

The Christian, on the other hand, sees this world in a very different perspective. It is like the desert which leads to the Promised Land. It is our place of exile, not our permanent home. It is the 'distant country' (Luke 15:13), far from our home and our waiting father. We know that we are not trapped by the world: we are *in* the world, but not *of* the world (John 17:13–19). We are committed to the world, because it is God's world for which Christ died, and because there is work to be done – but, in the end, we recognize that the world cannot be an end in itself. The world can too easily become a substitute for God. It is all too easy to allow the creation to subvert the place of the Creator. 'We are to learn to pass through this world as though it were a foreign country, treating all earthly things lightly and declining to set our hearts upon them' (John Calvin).

Think of your church or your Christian group as a 'colony of heaven'. Paul uses this idea when writing to the Christians at Philippi, a Roman colony (Philippians 3:20). A Roman colony was basically made up of a small group of Roman citizens, who had settled abroad. Although they were living in a strange and distant land, they kept the laws and customs of their homeland, they spoke its language, and longed for the day when they could return home. So it is with the Christian community. It is a colony of heaven on earth. Christians are 'aliens and strangers in the world' (1 Peter 2:11). Although it is set in the midst of hostile territory, its members keep the laws of heaven, and speak its language in worship and adoration. And they look forward to the day when they can return home to their native land, their exile finally ended.

'Since, then, you have been raised with Christ, set your hearts on things above, where Christ is seated at the right hand of God. Set your minds on things above, not on earthly things' (Colossians 3:1–2). With these words, Paul stresses the need for a *right perspective on life*. It is very easy for the believer, like anyone else, to get trapped in a rut. Work, family responsibilities, financial anxieties – all can become burdens which make us tired and weary. We look ahead, and see only more of the same sort of thing confronting us. It is very demoralizing! But it is here that Paul has some vital advice. Look upwards! Raise your head up, and look to the skies. Christ has ascended, blazing a trail in which we can follow. Thinking about the ascension is a helpful way of making sure that our outlook on life is right. It helps us recall that our destiny does not lie on this earth, but with the ascended Christ, who has gone ahead of us to prepare a place for us. He is waiting for us now. 'Our citizenship is in heaven' (Philippians 3:20). This gives a new perspective to the chores of everyday life. It sets before us a vision, which keeps us going. It is like an oasis in a desert – vital refreshment in the midst of the heat of life.

Key scriptural passages

Acts 1:1–11; Acts 2:32–36; Colossians 3:1–3.

Questions for discussion

Which do you think is the more important: the resurrection or the ascension?

How should we think about heaven?

How helpful is it to think of your Christian group as a 'colony of heaven'?

For further reading

Michael Green, *The Empty Cross of Jesus*. Includes discussion of the ascension, along with more detailed material relating to the resurrection.

Stephen Neill, *The Supremacy of Jesus*. Although not specifically concerned with the ascension itself, this is very helpful for thinking through the implications of the ascension for the supremacy and uniqueness of Jesus.

CHAPTER ELEVEN

He will come again to judge the living and the dead

HAVING dealt with Jesus in the past and the present, the Creed now points to the future: Jesus will one day return as judge of all, whether alive or dead at the time. Older English versions of the Creed use the phrase 'the quick and the dead'. 'Quick' is an Old English word for 'living', which still survives in words such as 'quicksilver' (mercury, which is a liquid metal at room temperature), and 'quicksands'.

The ideas explained

The basic idea encountered in the first part of this section is usually known as the 'second coming'. The Son of God, who once came to this earth in great humility, will one day come again in great glory. The saving plan of God, inaugurated in the first coming of Jesus Christ, will reach its grand finale with his second coming. The long-promised and awaited kingdom of God will be established. Perhaps the idea is expressed particularly well in Charles Wesley's famous hymn:

Lo, he comes with clouds descending,
Once for favoured sinners slain;
Thousand thousand saints attending
Swell the triumph of his train:
Alleluia! Christ appears on earth to reign.

The second idea to be dealt with is that of judgment. 'Man is destined to die once, and after that to face judgment' (Hebrews 9:27). Many people find the idea of judgment deeply threatening. I hope that the three points which follow may be helpful.

1. *We are being judged by someone who knows us totally.* We need not fear a superficial judgment, based upon an inadequate knowledge of us and our situation. Many of us manage to keep up an outward appearance which is very different from our real selves! Our public image often bears little relation to the way we really are. The advertising agencies and public relations media are often geared to projecting the image we want, and hiding the reality. While we may be able to fool other people, however, God is not taken in. The Old Testament emphasizes that God knows us totally (Psalm 139:1–4) – and loves us still. This theme is stressed especially in John's gospel: Jesus *knows* us. In his dealings with Nathanael (John 1:47–50), with the crowds (John 2:23–25) and with the Samaritan woman (John 4:18), we find the same pattern emerging: even before anyone tells Jesus anything about themselves, he already knows all about them.

For some people, this is a deeply disturbing thought. How awful that God sees through me like that! In fact, however, it ought to be a deeply reassuring thought. It means that we can be honest about ourselves with God, in a way that is impossible with other people. You might want to tell someone else about something that is troubling you – and they might respond, 'I never knew you were like that! I am deeply shocked.' God, however, knows us. He knows the reality that lies behind the facade.

2. *We are being judged by someone who is passionately committed to us.* The cross reveals God's love for us (John 3:16) as well as his judgment upon us. We are being judged by someone who cares for us, and is committed to us. Jesus himself was condemned by biased judges, hostile crowds and an indifferent public prosecutor: we shall be judged by one who cares deeply for us, and who is sympathetic towards us. It is deeply comforting to recall that our judge lived on this earth as one of us, and knows – at first hand – what we have to go through. He is not some far-off and distant figure, who has no understanding of our situation.

There is a magnificent story told about shepherds in East Anglia, the centre of England's wool trade in the Middle Ages. When a shepherd died, he would be buried in a coffin packed full of wool. The idea was that, when the day of judgment came, Jesus would see the wool, and realize that this man had been a shepherd. As he himself had once been a shepherd, he would know the pressures the man had faced – the amount of time needed to look after wayward sheep and so on – and would understand why he hadn't been to church much! The story makes an important point, in however amusing a manner, which we must treasure as one of the greatest of the many Christian insights into God. We are not dealing with a distant God who knows nothing of what being human means. He knows and understands – and so we can 'approach the throne of grace with confidence' (Hebrews 4:16).

3. *We are judged by someone who we know and trust.* We are already judged by our attitudes towards Jesus. Our response to the tender image of Christ dying upon the cross determines our attitude to God, and the results this brings in its wake. Jesus judges with the full authority of God. 'The Father loves the Son, and has placed everything in his hands. Whoever believes in the Son has eternal life, but whoever rejects the Son will not see life, for God's wrath remains upon him' (John 3:35–36). All authority on earth and in heaven has been granted to the risen Christ (Matthew 28:18), including the authority to judge. This is in no way inconsistent with the great Old Testament emphasis upon God as the sole judge of humanity. We saw earlier (p. 44) that only God can save – yet, on account of his divinity, Jesus saves. In the same way, only God can judge us – yet, on account of his divinity, Jesus judges us.

We are thus not judged on the basis of something unknown, but on the basis of our response to Jesus Christ. To believe in Jesus Christ is also to believe in the one who sent him – God the Father (John 12:44–45). Our attitude to Jesus determines our attitude to God, and hence the divine judgment upon us. That judgment is confirmed – not contradicted – at the last day. We have already been judged, and know the outcome of that judgment; what remains is the confirmation and enactment of that judgment. It is this idea which underlies the doctrine of justification by faith. 'Since we have been justified by faith, we have peace with God through our Lord Jesus Christ' (Romans 5:1). Faith is the basis of the divine judgment. However, as we saw earlier (p. 19), faith does not mean mere belief that God exists! Justifying faith is a trusting, obedient and transformative faith. 'The only thing that counts is faith expressing itself through love' (Galatians 5:6).

The ideas applied

'Do not judge, or you too will be judged. For in the same way as you judge others, you will be judged' (Matthew 7:1–2). Many Christians find themselves puzzled by these words. At first sight, they seem to suggest that Christians should *not* judge other people, Christians included. Yet on closer examination these, and other verses (*e.g.* Matthew 7:3–5) clearly suppose that Christians *do* judge others; they offer advice on *how* that judgment should be carried out. We all have a built-in tendency to be lenient and understanding when it comes to judging our own actions, and rather harsher and more censorious when it comes to judging those of others!

Criticism and judgment are an essential aspect of the life of the Christian community. It is a means of personal and communal growth. Without the criticism of others, each of us would become set in our ways, probably unaware of the negative and hurtful effect that our words and deeds can have on others. Criticism is a vital tool by which our own defects can be identified and corrected. Personal growth depends upon knowing what needs to be improved – and other Christians can help us in this way (Titus 2:15).

The passage from the Sermon on the Mount quoted above draws a clear connection between God's judgment of us, and our judgment of others. Our judgment of others should demonstrate the same pattern as God's judgment of us. In other words, God has set us an example in Jesus Christ of what Christian judgment should be like. See the gospel as God's criticism of us, which exposes us as sinners – but which opens the way to salvation.

1. *Criticism must be based on love and commitment to the other person.* Think of the cross of Christ, which shows both God's criticism of us and his love for us. In his love, God shows us what is wrong with us. But God doesn't just tell us that we are sinners, and leave us there! He offers to stand by us, and provide us with the resources we need if we are to be forgiven and grow in grace. In other words, he commits himself to be with us, supporting us as we respond to his criticism. Criticism is not an end in itself; it is the means to an end. God criticizes us in order to save us from ourselves.

The consequences of this are obvious. First, restrict your criticism to those you love and feel committed to. See criticism as presupposing commitment to the well-being of the other person. Second, don't let criticism become an end in itself. You must avoid criticizing people for the sake of it, or because it makes you feel good. Criticism must be directed towards the good of that person or the well-being of the Christian community as a whole. Third, be prepared to help your friends. There is no point in criticizing anyone unless you are prepared to stand by them and help them if they accept and respond to your criticism. Your criticism must also be an offer of help. Don't just say, 'You irritate people.' Rather, say something like, 'I care for you, and as a result, I think I ought to tell you that you irritate people. But I can help you deal with this one. Will you let me?'

2. *Criticism must be informed.* One of the reasons why it is easy to take criticism from God is that we trust his

judgment. He is fully informed. He knows us. But your criticism of your friends may not be informed. You may not be completely in the picture. You may not wholly understand their situation. You may lack experience of the sorts of situations they're in. It's very easy to criticize someone from the outside. Take time to understand your friends, just as you would like them to take time to understand you. Understanding people doesn't mean you can give up criticizing them – but it does mean that your criticism will be informed and helpful – and less frequent!

Finally, before you criticize anyone, take a good look at yourself! You may not share exactly the same problem as your friend – but there may be others there instead. Criticism of others should presuppose criticism of yourself (Matthew 7:3–5). If you feel you must criticize anyone, why not invite them to criticize you in return? That way, both of you may grow in faith and love.

Key scriptural passages

Matthew 25:31–46; Acts 10:42; 1 Thessalonians 4:13 – 5:11; 2 Peter 3:3–10.

Questions for discussion

Is God's judgment a totally future event? Or does it begin in the present?

Have you ever found criticism from others helpful? positively unhelpful?

Who would you feel able to take criticism from?

For further reading

Ray S. Anderson, *Theology, Death and Dying*, pp. 64–81. A useful account of some of the issues raised by divine judgment, aimed mainly at an academic readership.

C. S. Lewis, *The Great Divorce*. A fine literary allegory, which weaves together many of the threads of the Christian understanding of judgment. Entertaining and thought-provoking.

Stephen H. Travis, *The Jesus Hope*, pp. 46–68. Eminently readable account of the themes of this section.

CHAPTER TWELVE

I believe in the Holy Spirit

THE Trinitarian structure of the Creed is now completed. Having dealt with faith in God the Father and God the Son, the Creed turns to deal with the Holy Spirit.

The idea explained

In both of the main biblical languages – Hebrew in the Old Testament, and Greek in the New – the words for 'wind', 'breath' and 'spirit' are the same. It is very easy for the English reader, unaware of these associations, to miss the full richness of the biblical witness to the person and work of the Holy Spirit (for example, see John 3:6–8 for wordplay on 'wind' and 'Spirit'). To gain some insights into the vitality of the biblical understanding of the Spirit of God, we shall consider briefly two ideas.

1. *The Spirit brings life.* When God created Adam, he breathed into him the breath of life, as a result of which he became a living being (Genesis 2:7). The basic difference between a living and a dead human being is that the former breathes, and the latter does not. God is the one who breathes the breath of life

into empty shells, and brings them to life. Just as God brought Adam to life by breathing into him, so God is able to bring individuals and his church to life through his Spirit today. The famous vision of the valley of the dry bones (Ezekiel 37:1–14) also illustrates this point – the bones only come to life when breath enters into them (Ezekiel 37:9–10). The Spirit, then, can be thought of as God bringing new life to his creation.

2. *The Spirit brings power.* All of us are used to seeing things being moved by an invisible force – the wind. We often see papers blown across the road by the wind, or trees bending before its force. And in those areas of the world where hurricanes or tornadoes are common, entire towns may be destroyed by the power of this invisible force which we call the wind. And the Old Testament writers, noticing the way in which the wind acted, could hardly fail to notice an obvious parallel with the way in which God acted. The Spirit of God is like the wind – an unseen force which acts upon things and people. The Spirit can be thought of as God in action.

These images, then, help us begin to think about what the Holy Spirit is like. The wind and human breath are invaluable visual aids for thinking about the Spirit. But what does the Spirit do? What do Christians believe about him? We have only enough space to hit the high points of the richness of the Christian understanding of the work of the Spirit; much more could – and should – be said.

1. *The Holy Spirit convicts us of our sin.* It is a mammoth, indeed superhuman, task to convince people that they really are sinners. Yet we are not alone in this task. God gives a gift which is equal to the task. Jesus promised his disciples the continued presence

and power of the Spirit after he had left them. The Spirit would convict the world of its guilt and sin, and convince them of the reality of judgment (John 16:7–11). The practical outworking of this may be seen in Peter's great Pentecost sermon, when all barriers of language were broken down in order that individuals might be confronted with and convicted of their sins (Acts 2:1–13; 37–41).

2. *The Holy Spirit is a pledge of our salvation.* God 'put his Spirit in our hearts as a deposit, guaranteeing what is to come' (2 Corinthians 1:22; *cf.* 2 Corinthians 5:5; Ephesians 1:14). The Greek word for 'deposit' – *arrabōn* – is often translated as 'pledge' or 'surety'. It is an unusual word, probably deriving from Phoenician traders. Its basic meaning is a 'down payment', or a 'token of commitment'. In many hire-purchase agreements, the buyer has to put down a deposit or a down payment to secure possession of the item; that deposit promises that there is more payment to come, and also ensures possession of the item. God places his Spirit within our hearts as a down payment: it demonstrates that we are his, and promises that there is more to come. It is a surety or pledge of our salvation.

VITAL TRUTH

3. *The Holy Spirit is our comforter.* As Jesus prepares to leave his disciples, he promises to send them a comforter (John 14:25–26) – the Holy Spirit. The Greek word *paraklētos* is usually translated as 'comforter', 'advocate' or 'counsellor'. (Incidentally, if you are used to singing very old hymns, you may come across reference to the 'Paraclete' – this is simply a way of referring to the Holy Spirit.) The Spirit will comfort the disciples by reminding them of Jesus (John 14:26; 15:26). He will bring them peace.

In 1066, Norman armies under Willam the Conqueror successfully invaded England. That event was commemorated in the Bayeaux Tapestry, a remarkably detailed record of the events of that campaign. One of its scenes depicts a column of Norman soldiers on horseback. They are followed by the Bishop of Bayeaux, who is busy poking the last man with a large stick. The caption to this little scene reads: 'Bishop Odo comforts the soldiers.' Most of us would feel that this is the sort of comfort that we could well do without! Yet the Greek word for 'comfort' can bear the meaning 'urge on', or 'encourage to do greater things'. There is a sense in which the Spirit does prod us, encouraging and empowering us to do things which we otherwise would not – and could not – do.

The idea applied

Many Christians feel anxious over the question of spiritual gifts. They read passages such as 1 Corinthians 12:1–11, and feel that they lack these spiritual gifts. They wonder if they are second-class Christians as a result; some even wonder if they really are Christians! It is important to make the crucial distinction between the *fruit* of the Spirit – such as joy, peace and love – (Galatians 5:22) and the *gifts* of the Spirit. Think of two trees. One is an apple tree. If it really is an apple tree, it ought to bear apples. You know it by its fruit (Matthew 12:33). Similarly, Christians ought to show the fruit of the Spirit in their lives, although the extent will vary from one person to another.

Now think of two fir trees. One is growing in a forest. The other is a Christmas tree, inside a home and covered with presents. Those presents have nothing to do with the tree! They didn't grow there. They were placed there by someone. They are someone's gifts, not the natural fruit of the tree. Not every fir tree becomes a Christmas tree and gets covered with presents – but that doesn't deny that they are fir trees! Spiritual gifts are *gifts*. God gives them to those who he feels need them, or who he feels can use them especially well. But they are not all given to everyone! It is no stigma to lack a charisma!

And if you have been entrusted with spiritual gifts, try to see them in the right way and use them wisely. To start with, remember that gifts are gifts, not rewards. 'What do you have that you did not receive?' (1 Corinthians 4:7). Furthermore, remember that God gives gifts for a purpose – they aren't there for ornament, but are meant to be used 'for the common good' (1 Corinthians 12:7). The Parable of the Talents (Matthew 25:14–30) makes this point especially well. The parable tells of a master who entrusts his money to some servants during his absence, and of the variety of ways in which the servants make use of that money. There are three main points being made by this parable, all of which are important.

1. *Our talents are gifts from God.* The servants had no claim on the money: it was their master's, entrusted to them during his absence. In one sense, it was a gift to them – but a gift which they would eventually have to surrender. They were stewards, rather than possessors, of the money. They were responsible for its wise use during the master's absence. In much the same way, we have been entrusted with gifts from God – not on account of

our personal worthiness, but on account of the tasks and responsibilities which God may have in mind for us. The important thing is to identify what your particular gifts might be, as the first step in using them in God's service.

2. *God's gifts are given in order to be used.* You mustn't think of spiritual gifts as some kind of ornament, there just to decorate you and make you a more interesting person! They are there to be used, in the building up of the people of God and the furthering of his kingdom. In the parable, the returning master is furious with the servant who buried his talent, and refused to use it. Some Christians adopt this ostrich-like approach to spiritual gifts, ignoring them or failing to use them. Spiritual gifts are task-orientated, there for a purpose. They are all on loan. We are responsible for expending them in the world, and we will be held accountable for the way in which we use them.

3. *God's gifts increase through being used.* The parable tells of three servants, two of whom use their talents, and the third who buries it in the ground. This final talent remains unaltered in its hole in the ground. It was not used and therefore did not grow. The two other servants, however, found that the money with which they had been entrusted increased through being used wisely. And so it is with the spiritual gifts which God gives us.

So if you have spiritual gifts, make sure you use them; if you do not, you need not be anxious. You may have genuine gifts and talents of a different sort; it may be that God will bestow a spiritual gift upon you later in life, to meet a specific situation. If in doubt, you may find it helpful to pray for discernment. But there is no need for anxiety – simply honesty!

Key scriptural passages

John 14:15–27; Acts 2:1–21; 1 Corinthians 14:1–25.

Questions for discussion

How is it helpful to think of the Spirit as: wind? breath?

In what ways does the Spirit empower us in our lives?

How might you discern your spiritual gifts in the first place?

For further reading

Michael Green, *I believe in the Holy Spirit*. A first-rate introduction to the subject. Thoroughly recommended.

Michael Ramsey, *Holy Spirit*. A fine study by a former Archbishop of Canterbury. Particularly helpful for those already with some knowledge of the subject.

Tom Smail, *Reflected Glory*. A very readable introduction to the person and work of the Holy Spirit.

CHAPTER THIRTEEN

The holy catholic church

WE now come to faith in the church, the body of Christ. To believe in Jesus Christ is to believe in, and to belong to, a dynamic community which spans the centuries.

The ideas explained

The Greek word *ekklēsia*, used in the New Testament to refer to the church, does not denote a building, but a group of people. It literally means 'those who are called out'. The church consists of those who have been called out of the world into a community of faith – those who God has 'called out of darkness into his wonderful light' (1 Peter 2:9). To become a Christian is to enter into this community of support, encouragement and love.

It is traditional to speak of the 'four marks of the church' – in other words, four characteristic identifying features. The Creed here notes two, implies one more, and omits reference to a fourth. For the sake of fullness, we shall consider all four.

1. *The church is one*. This is implied by the Creed, which speaks of 'the church', not 'churches'. All

Christian churches are based and founded on the one and only foundation of Jesus Christ himself. There is no other foundation upon which they can stand. We could say that the Christian church is that body of people which acknowledges Jesus Christ as its head (Colossians 1:18). Even a casual glance at modern Western society shows that there are many different churches or denominations. Yet, to the extent that these are genuinely Christian, they are all part of the one church. The disunity of the churches does not deny the fact that the church is one.

In recent years, under increasing pressure from secular society, many Christian churches have come to realize that what they have in common is far more precious and important than what divides them. There is a growing recognition that Christians are at liberty to disagree over certain matters – things that are not essential to the gospel – while taking a common stand on the essentials of the gospel. For example, I am an Anglican – but it is of infinitely greater importance to me that I am a *Christian* than that I am an Anglican. 'There is one body and one Spirit – just as you were called to one hope when you were called – one Lord, one faith, one baptism, one Father of all, who is over all and through all and in all' (Ephesians 4:4–6).

2. *The church is holy*. 'Holy' is a word which turns most people off. It suggests sanctimoniousness, or a 'holier than thou' attitude. To some, it even suggests that the church is full of self-satisfied bores. And is the church *really* holy? C. S. Lewis documents this attitude well in *The Screwtape Letters*, in which the new convert goes to church, expecting to find it full of saints – and instead discovers it is full of ordinary

people like himself! But to understand this aspect of the church, we need to recover the true meaning of the word 'holy'. This point is so important that we shall reserve discussion of it for the following chapter, in which we deal in depth with 'the communion of saints'.

3. *The church is catholic.* Many people find this part of the Creed difficult to accept. Since the time of the European Reformation of the sixteenth century, many people have come to use the word 'catholic' to mean 'Roman Catholic'. In fact, this isn't implied. The Greek word *katholikos* means 'according to the whole', or 'universal'. If I were to say that a friend of mine has 'a catholic taste', I don't mean that he prefers to attend a requiem mass rather than a prayer meeting! It just means that his taste is very wide, taking in a broad range. In saying that the church is catholic, we are affirming that its message is valid and relevant to every age and every situation. It is not as if there is one church with a message suited to the needs of the second century, and another with a message suited to the needs of the twentieth – it is the same church, throughout the ages and across the world, which seeks to apply the same gospel in whatever situation it may happen to meet. It is an affirmation of the universal validity and relevance of the gospel.

4. *The church is apostolic.* In other words, it continues steadfastly in the faith and teaching of the first apostles (Acts 2:42), and gladly accepts the great commission entrusted to them (Matthew 28:16–20). The faith and the tasks of the apostles have become ours. 'The faith that was once for all entrusted to the saints' (Jude 3) has now been entrusted to us for a time, before we pass it on to

those who will follow us. We, and all other Christians, are stewards of the same gospel once entrusted to the apostles.

Taken together, these four 'marks of the church' point to a world-wide body of believers, whose sole foundation is Jesus Christ, who have been entrusted with the apostles' faith and responsibilities to proclaim the gospel throughout history, knowing that it is of continued vital relevance to the human race.

The ideas applied

To believe in the church is to recognize the need for support structures for faith. Individual Christians are not meant to exist on their own – they are meant to be part of a community. Cyprian of Carthage, a famous early Christian martyr, once wrote: 'No-one can have God as his father who does not have the church for his mother.' In other words, to acknowledge God as our Father means joining a community of people who share that faith, and whose historical roots lie firmly in the New Testament. While stressing the importance of a personal faith, the New Testament has no time for individualism, whether of the eccentric type which led some to become cave-dwelling hermits in days of old, or of a more modern kind which stresses self-sufficiency.

The world is an increasingly hostile place for faith to exist. As early as 1942, the greatly respected English writer C. S. Lewis described faith as existing on 'enemy territory'. Writing during the Second World War, when much of continental Europe was occupied by Nazi armies, Lewis suggested that faith was like a resistance movement which was fighting an invading power – secularism. That invading power was determined to stamp out any resistance which it met. Since then, Western culture has become much more aggressively secular. Those committed to secular values have a vested interest in destroying the credibility of the Christian faith – and that means *your* personal faith as well. Many Christians find the new aggressiveness of secular culture deeply disturbing. It seems to call their faith into question. The hostility of much of modern Western society seems very threatening. It causes many Christians to become despondent. At best, the world seems indifferent to their faith; at worst, it treats it as absurd.

It is very common for Christians to find themselves isolated at work, or ridiculed for their faith. They are very conscious of the fact that their faith marks them out as 'abnormal' in the eyes of their colleagues. It's almost as if you have to apologize for believing in God. Christian values and presuppositions are gradually being squeezed out of every area of modern Western culture. 'Christianity is a fighting religion' (C. S. Lewis). Faith, like a resistance movement, has to survive in a very hostile environment.

But it *can* survive – and it survives best in community, rather than in isolation. Try to think yourself into the situation faced by the first Christians during the New Testament period. They were faced with hostility on every side. They were ridiculed as fools. They were very few in number. Try to think yourself into their situation, and imagine how incredibly despondent you might feel about it! Yet the first Christians were not unduly worried by these problems. They weren't overwhelmed by the hostility of their environment. The resurrection of

Jesus set those difficulties in perspective. The God who raised Jesus from the dead was with them, and on their side. And they had each other for support and encouragement.

We should not feel intimidated or threatened either. In fact, the new hostility of secular culture to the gospel makes it easier for us to identify with the Christian communities we read about in the New Testament letters. Their situation is very like ours, in many respects. So take comfort from the experience of the early Christians, and let yourself be inspired and encouraged by their words and examples. And, above all, let their concern for living out the faith in a community, in a church, affect the way you live.

So appreciate the pastoral importance of support groups. Make sure you don't get isolated, and have to cope with the pressures placed on you by society on your own. You need to be encouraged by other Christians. You need to spend time with other people whose 'world-view' is the same as yours. This is particularly important for Christian students at college or university, where pressure from secular beliefs and values can be considerable. It is also important for professionals in any field, where it is common for Christians to feel under pressure to conform to prevailing professional codes of ethics, rather than an obligation to obey the gospel. Time and time again, the gospel and such codes of ethics can come into conflict. You need to *be supported* by others, and you need to *support* others. The world aims to isolate you, to demoralize you, to break down your confidence in yourself and the gospel (read John 17:14–18). You need to be able to discuss problems you have in common – such as how to cope with the pressure brought on Christians by society in general, by your colleagues at work, or by your family and friends in particular. Don't just *go* to church – *get involved* in home groups, Bible study groups, special interest groups, houseparties or camps. Encourage your fellow-Christians, and let them encourage you. Think of the church as your extended family, somewhere you can *belong*.

Finally, a word of warning. As historians have pointed out, it is very easy for faith in Jesus Christ to degenerate into loyalty to a church. Somehow Jesus seems to recede into the background, as the *institution* of the church becomes of paramount importance. Loyalty to a specific denomination, or even devotion to a specific building, can come to be of greater importance than loyalty to Jesus Christ. Try to keep things in perspective!

Key scriptural passages

1 Corinthians 12:4–31; Ephesians 5:25–33; Colossians 1:18.

Questions for discussion

Is belief in the church an optional extra for Christians?

What ideas are suggested by referring to the church as 'the body of Christ'?

Is it helpful to think of the church as 'the Christian family'?

For further reading

David Jackman, *Understanding the Church*. A useful guide to the complexities of the church, at both the theoretical and practical levels.

Hans Küng, *The Church*. An excellent introduction to the theory of the church. Written from a Roman Catholic perspective, it contains many helpful insights.

David Watson, *I believe in the Church*. An excellent and highly readable guide to the subject. Highly recommended.

CHAPTER FOURTEEN

The communion of saints

IN the previous section, we looked at some aspects of the Christian understanding of the church. The present section allows us to examine one feature of this in more detail. The previous chapter dealt with the church as a body; we are now concerned with ourselves as members of that body.

The ideas explained

As we saw, the New Testament writers never use the word 'church' with buildings in mind. When Paul writes to the churches at Corinth or Galatia, for example (1 Corinthians 1:2; Galatians 1:2), he is writing to groups of people, not to a building. (The early Christians had no special buildings of their own, set apart for worship; they seem to have met in each others' homes.) The 'church' is not a static building, but a dynamic pilgrim people who are constantly moving on in faith and obedience. It includes those who have gone ahead of us, and those who will follow. It is a great fellowship of faith, spanning the ages and the continents. The Creed now develops this aspect of the Christian understanding of the church. 'Communion' is the old English word for 'fellowship' – and that identifies a key role of the church. Among its many functions, the church is there to support its members.

What does 'fellowship' mean? The Greek word used in the New Testament to express this idea (*koinōnia*) has the basic meaning of 'sharing'. At one level, it means 'sharing joys and sorrows'. It is usually much easier to cope with sadness if you are able to share it with someone else. He or she may be able to offer you good advice, or even practical assistance – but somehow, even the act of sharing a problem often seems to work wonders. Knowing that someone else is remembering your difficulties in their prayers can be of enormous comfort. Those who are strong in the faith and rich in spiritual gifts have responsibilities towards those who are weak in the faith, and who lack these talents. God's gifts are given for the building up, or edification, of the Christian community (1 Corinthians 14:3–5) – and that implies a willingess to share them.

But fellowship operates at another level (Romans 12:13; Ephesians 4:28; 1 Timothy 6:18; Hebrews 13:16). It operates at the level of material goods and wealth. The apostles held all things in common (Acts 2:44–45). Each gave according to his or her ability, and each received according to his or her need. There is no need to confuse this with secular socialist philosophies. It is a reminder of the need for mutual commitment within the Christian fellowship. Those who are strong have responsibilities towards those who are weak, just as those who are rich have responsibilities towards those who are poor. In the early Christian communities, widows and orphans were singled out as needing special care and compassion (*e.g.* Acts 6:1; James 1:27). To believe in the 'fellowship of saints' is to be committed to the practical consequences of this fellowship.

Paul often begins his letters by addressing the 'saints' – whether at Rome (Romans 1:4), Corinth (2 Corinthians 1:1) or Ephesus (Ephesians 1:1). But what is a saint? Groucho Marx once remarked that he wouldn't want to join a club that would have him as a member! Many of us feel the same way about the church as a fellowship of saints. If *I* am a saint, then there is nothing special about it! If all believers are saints, the idea of a saint seems to be devalued. Perhaps it is natural that some people find this a genuine problem. The two lines of argument which follow may be helpful.

First, the word 'saint' just means 'someone who is holy'. Christians are holy, not because of anything they are in themselves, but because of the one who has called them. The fact that we are holy has nothing to do with our personal merit or sanctity of life; it has everything to do with the fact that we have been called by a holy God, and have responded to him. We are holy because of our calling, not because of our natures. Think of the moon, which shines by reflecting the light of the sun. As the Apollo moon mission of the 1960s made clear, the moon is a dead world. It possesses no light of its own. But it can reflect the light of the sun. Christians are holy in much the same way as the moon shines at night – by reflecting something (or someone) else. God's holiness can be reflected in our lives, even if we ourselves are sinners.

To declare that we believe in the 'communion of saints' does not mean that we believe in a holy club; it means that we believe in a holy God who has called us as individuals into a community, within which his work of renewal and regeneration can take place. To be called by God is deeply humbling, and is not in any way a cause for pride or arrogance. God calls us while we are sinners into a community within which his work of healing can begin. We are called *to be* holy (1 Corinthians 1:2), not because we *are* holy. 'It is not the healthy who need a doctor, but the sick. I have not come to call the righteous, but sinners' (Mark 2:17). Augustine of Hippo, a great Christian writer of the late fourth and early fifth centuries, remarked that the church was rather like a hospital. It was full of sick people, who were desperately hoping to be cured. The church is a fellowship of forgiven sinners, who confidently hope, by God's grace, to become a fellowship of saints.

Second, think of a saint – and hence of yourself – as someone who is consecrated to God. Let's explore this idea, and see how it helps. The basic meaning of 'consecration' is 'being set apart'. Think of a communion service. At some point during the service, the bread and the wine are *consecrated*. The bread and wine remain bread and wine; but they are set apart to serve a special purpose. The words spoken by Jesus at the Last Supper are recalled, as his commandment to 'do this in remembrance of me' (Luke 22:19). Then, shortly afterwards, they are distributed to the members of the congregation. The bread and the wine are meant to remind believers of the suffering and death of Jesus Christ, upon which our salvation rests.

Consecration means being set apart to remind people of Jesus Christ. We do not suddenly become holy and righteous; indeed, sin remains a major threat to our Christians lives. But despite our sin, we have been set apart from the world. We have been called out of that world (remember that we saw that the Greek word for 'church' means 'called out') in order to remind that world of its Saviour and Lord. Being members of the 'communion of saints' means that we have been called from the world to proclaim the saving love of God for that world.

So there is no problem in speaking of the church as 'the communion of saints'. Of course it is a 'fellowship of sinners' as well! But it is a fellowship of *forgiven* sinners, who are in the process of *becoming* holy. The German reformer Martin Luther taught that Christians are 'righteous and sinners at one and the same time (*simul iustus et peccator*)'. We are righteous on account of God having clothed us with his righteousness – but inside, we are still sinners. God justifies us on the basis of his gift of righteousness, rather than on the basis of any righteousness which we may possess. Although we are sinners, God is still able to renew and regenerate our fallen natures. Just as workmen on a building site might cover their work with tarpaulins to protect it from the elements, so God shelters his work of renewal and regeneration within us with the external covering of his righteousness. Although we remain sinners externally, we thus live in hope, knowing that God is at work within us, renewing and rebuilding us from within. Luther argues that justified sinners are like people who are ill, yet who have been entrusted to the care of a competent physician. They are righteous 'not in fact, but in hope (*non in re sed in spe*)'. The signs of recovery and sanctification within us point to our future perfection in righteousness, just as a patient under the care of a good physician can rest assured of being cured as he detects signs of recovery.

Nevertheless, most of us know of some individuals

– whether historical figures from the past, or people now living – who have deeply impressed us by their faith, their quality of life, and their faithful devotion to God. Somehow, it seems right to speak of them as 'saints' in some special way. The witness of their lives is both an encouragement and a challenge: an encouragement, because it demonstrates what God can indeed do and achieve with fallen human nature; and a challenge, because we have yet to allow him to do this with us!

The ideas applied

Draw comfort and support from others! That is one of the practical consequences of the doctrine of the 'communion of saints'. Read Hebrews 11:1 – 12:3, and realize that you share in the faith of these great figures of old. You all belong to the same great family. They have all been through the trials, struggles and tempations of faith before you. They are now 'a great cloud of witnesses' (Hebrews 12:1) cheering you on, as you run the same race. Try to visualize the scene, as you think of a great Roman amphitheatre, with the racecourse ahead of you, and the crowds shouting their support and encouragement as you aim to complete the race, and gain your crown of laurel.

You can draw encouragement from the past in other ways. It can often be helpful to attempt to draw up a spiritual family tree. Try to identify the people who were important in helping you come to faith. Perhaps one person was of vital importance; perhaps several people helped you come to faith gradually, over a long period of time. But remember that each of them was helped to faith by someone! And each of them by someone else! Perhaps you could find out who they were. And by doing this, you will discover a vast network of faithful believers, most of whom are now dead, who have contributed in some way to bringing you to faith. That's what the 'communion of saints' is all about. It is a vast network of faithful individuals, who play their part in working out God's purposes. You share in that faith, and you share in that work.

Key scriptural passages

Acts 4:32–37; Romans 12:3–11; Ephesians 4:11–16; Hebrews 11:1 – 12:3.

Questions for discussion

What factors are important in establishing good fellowship?

In what ways are Christians holy?

Try to identify individuals who have helped you in your life of faith.

For further reading

J. C. Ryle, *Holiness*. A classic, dating from the nineteenth century. Full of insights into the struggle for holiness.

Derek Tidball, *Skilful Shepherds*, pp. 247–338. An excellent guide to the various pastoral skills needed in developing and deepening fellowship.

David Watson, *I believe in the Church*. Full of helpful insights on fellowship and its implications.

CHAPTER FIFTEEN

The forgiveness of sins

IN this brief section, the Creed compresses its understanding of what Jesus Christ achieved on the cross. No attempt is made to explain the idea, or elaborate upon it. However, in this terse phrase we are to find summarized the full richness of the New Testament understanding of the work of Jesus Christ.

The idea explained

The New Testament uses a wide range of images to express the richness of its understanding of the work of Christ. The 'forgiveness of sins' is mentioned as an example of these images, and is not meant to exhaust them! The Nicene Creed – a somewhat longer and more detailed version of the Creed – adds to this brief statement, telling us that Jesus Christ became man 'for our salvation', adding another image to that of forgiveness. Taken together, these biblical images of the achievement of Jesus Christ aim to explain what was going on between God, Christ and sinful humanity in the crucifixion and resurrection of Jesus. What is remarkable about these images is that they are able to explain the complexity of the achievement of Jesus Christ in terms or ideas which we already know from everyday life. The New Testament writers did exactly what every good preacher is meant to do – use illustrations and analogies drawn from their experience to help 'unpack' their theology. To fully understand what happened on the cross, we have to follow the New Testament carefully, as it builds up a picture of what was going on by using a wide range of illustrations, each of which casts light on one particular aspect of our subject. It may well be that one individual finds one illustration more helpful than another – but this does not entitle him to argue that it is this illustration, and this illustration alone, which is good enough to stand on its own as a description of what was going on. Let us begin by looking at four images the New Testament uses to bring out the meaning of the death and resurrection of Jesus Christ.

1. *Forgiveness of sins*. It is no accident that the Creed selects this image to summarize the work of Christ. It is perhaps the most powerful and familiar image used to explain the significance of Christ's death and resurrection for believers. The image can be interpreted in two ways: legally and personally. The legal use of the term is probably most familiar from the Parable of the Merciless Servant (Matthew 18:23–35). Here forgiveness is understood in terms of the remission of a debt. The idea of 'forgiveness of sins' may thus be regarded as a legal concept, involving the remission of a penalty or debt. Jesus wiped out our guilt by his death on the cross. Whatever penalty was due for human sin has been fully met by the obedient death of Christ upon the cross.

The second sense of the term is closely related to the idea of 'reconciliation'. Forgiveness is what is necessary for a personal relationship to be restored to its former state after a hurtful disagreement or misunderstanding. Forgiveness involves someone taking the initiative. If there are two persons who once enjoyed a close relationship, but now have drifted apart, that relationship will remain broken unless someone attempts a reconciliation. Someone has to take the initiative, and approach the other party, acknowledging that the relationship has gone wrong, recalling how precious and important that relationship once was, affirming their love and concern for the other – and asking them to restore the relationship. If the other party is not prepared to restore the relationship, no progress has been made. If forgiveness is offered but not accepted, the relationship remains unaltered. If, and only if, both parties agree to restore the relationship will forgiveness be achieved. There must be a decision to *accept* God's forgiveness on our part. All this is evident from our own experience of personal relationships. By making an appeal to personal relationships, the New Testament grounds our relationship with God in everyday experience.

We could say that sin is what comes between us and God, and threatens to wreck our relationship with him. 'Your iniquities have separated you from your God' (Isaiah 59:2). Sin is a barrier erected from our side between ourselves and God. Our sin separates us from God. The Creed, however, affirms a central and joyous insight of the New Testament – this barrier *can* be broken down, and *has* been broken down by God.

At the moment of Jesus' death, the curtain of the

temple at Jerusalem was torn down (Matthew 27:51). The curtain prevented ordinary people from gaining access to the innermost part of the temple. It seemed to deny them access to the presence of God. In the tearing of that curtain at the moment of Jesus' death, many commentators see the full meaning of that death dramatically symbolized. The barrier between human beings and God has been broken down by the death of Jesus Christ. To believe in the forgiveness of sins is to believe that God can break down all the barriers between us and him – if we will let him.

2. *Reconciliation.* 'God was reconciling the world to himself in Christ' (2 Corinthians 5:19). This famous statement draws our attention to the idea of 'reconciliation'. The word and the idea are very familiar. Reconciliation is fundamental to human experience, especially in the area of personal relationships. The Parable of the Prodigal Son (Luke 15:11–32) is perhaps the supreme illustration of the importance of reconciliation in the New Testament. It illustrates vividly the reconciliation of father and son, and the restoration of their broken relationship. As with forgiveness, we note that reconciliation offered, but not accepted, fails to heal a broken relationship. God offers us reconciliation through the death of Jesus Christ; we must accept that offer if our relationship with him is to be healed and transformed.

3. *Salvation.* This idea is used frequently in the New Testament (*e.g.* Acts 13:26; Ephesians 1:13; Hebrews 1:14) to express the basic idea of deliverance, preservation, or rescue, from a dangerous situation. The verb is used outside the New Testament to refer to being saved from death by the intervention of a rescuer, or to being cured from a

deadly illness. It can also refer to being kept in good health. The word 'salvation' is thus used by the Jewish historian Josephus to refer to the deliverance of the Israelites from Egyptian bondage.

'Salvation' expresses two central notions. The first idea is that of being rescued or delivered from a dangerous situation. For example, the Israelites were delivered from their captivity in Egypt at the time of the Exodus. In the same way, Christ is understood to deliver us from the fear of death and the power of sin. The name 'Jesus' means 'God saves' – and it is clear that the New Testament means 'saves *from sin*' (Matthew 1:21). Secondly, it points to the idea of 'wholeness' or 'health'. Thus it is sometimes difficult to know whether a passage should be translated in terms of salvation or wholeness – for example, should the Greek version of Mark 5:34 be translated as 'Your faith has made you whole' or 'Your faith has saved you?' When someone who has been ill is healed, he or she is restored to his or her former state of health, of wholeness. The creation stories of Genesis make it clear that God created people in a state of wholeness, and that this wholeness was lost through the Fall. Just as healing involves restoring someone to health, so salvation involves restoring human wholeness, restoring us to the state in which we were first created by God. In many respects the gospel is like a medicine – something which heals us.

4. *Redemption.* To redeem something is to buy it back. When Paul uses the word, he is thinking of the redemption of slaves, a familiar event in New Testament times. A slave could redeem himself by buying his freedom. The word used to describe this event could literally be translated as 'being taken out of the slave market'. The word expresses the idea of

restoring someone to a state of liberty – at a price. Christ's death and resurrection set us free from our bondage to sin and death. Paul's repeated emphasis that Christians are slaves who have been 'bought at a price' (1 Corinthians 6:20; 7:23) makes the full force of the idea of redemption clear: we have been freed from bondage to sin only at the cost of the death of Jesus Christ. Real redemption is something precious and costly, God's greatest gift to his people.

These, then, are some of the ways in which the New Testament speaks of the meaning of the death of Christ for believers. Their full richness, complemented by that of other images not discussed here, is called to mind by the section of the Creed we have just considered.

The idea applied

Real forgiveness is a costly and precious thing. It is far easier to pretend to forgive someone – you can just paper over the cracks and ignore the real problems. But real forgiveness goes to the heart of the problem. It identifies the cause of the hurt and pain between two people. It is difficult for both the forgiver and the forgiven. For the forgiver, it means trying to cope with the pain and offence caused by the other. It means recognizing that healing of the relationship must take precedence over personal injury and slight. Many people find it painfully difficult to forgive someone who has really hurt them. It is easy to forgive someone for something trivial. When that person has really wounded you, it is much more difficult. Try, then, to imagine how difficult it is for God to forgive us. Try to understand how much God must love us if he is prepared to do this. The fact that we find it so difficult to forgive people at times brings home to us how marvellous a thing divine forgiveness is.

For the forgiven, it involves admitting that something is wrong, and taking responsibility for it. It means coming to terms with the considerable hurt that we may have caused someone else. It involves humility and repentance, and a willingness to try and avoid causing such hurt in future. It is no wonder that many people find forgiveness so difficult! But it brings renewal of a relationship which would otherwise be lost, or become meaningless. God's offer of forgiveness affirms how much we matter to him. Condemnation and love are mingled in that gracious and precious offer, made to us through the cross. The sins of the past are set firmly behind us, as forgiven, in order that we may turn in humble confidence to the future of faith.

Having considered how costly true forgiveness is, we must then come to terms with the gospel demand that we too should be forgiving. There is a sense in which God's forgiveness of our sins depends upon our forgiving those who sin against us (Matthew 6:14–15; 18:23–35). We must forgive as the Lord forgave us (Colossians 3:13). An unwillingness to forgive others can be a serious obstacle to personal growth (it is so easy to harbour grudges for ages), and can also threaten the unity of the Christian community. 'Be forgiving' is no easy platitude; it is essential to the well-being of individuals and communities.

Key scriptural passages

Isaiah 59:1–15; Matthew 18:23–35; 2 Corinthians 5:18–21; 1 Peter 1:14–17.

Questions for discussion

What additional biblical images of the work of Christ can you think of?

Why is forgiveness essential to the healing of personal relationships?

Why is real forgiveness so difficult to accept?

For further reading

Francis Schaeffer, *True Spirituality*, pp. 93–147. An excellent account of the importance of forgiveness for spiritual growth and healing.

John Stott, *The Cross of Christ*. A superb account of the meaning of the cross of Jesus, developing many of the themes of this chapter.

Derek Tidball, *Skilful Shepherds*, pp. 266–279. A careful study of the pastoral importance of forgiveness.

CHAPTER SIXTEEN

The resurrection of the body, and the life everlasting. Amen.

THE Creed ends on a positive note, with a clear statement of the Christian hope. The Creed opened with a statement of faith in God; it now ends with a statement of hope that we shall one day stand in the presence of that same God.

The ideas explained

The Creed links together two ideas, as it gives expression to the Christian hope. Earlier, it proclaimed the reality of the resurrection of Jesus Christ; now, it affirms the common Christian hope that all believers will one day share in his glorious resurrection. Christians will be where Jesus now is. Jesus' words to his disciples, as the hour of his own death drew near, are very important here. 'Do not let your hearts be troubled. Trust in God; trust also in me. In my Father's house are many rooms ... I am going there to prepare a place for you. And if I go and prepare a place for you, I will come back and take you to be with me that you may also be where I am' (John 14:1–3).

What is the connection between the resurrection of

Jesus and our future resurrection? It is helpful to consider the idea of adoption in exploring this point. Paul uses this legal image for two purposes (Romans 8:15; 8:23; 9:4; Galatians 4:5; Ephesians 1:5). First, it expresses the difference between 'sons of God' (believers) and *the* Son of God (Jesus Christ). A father would be free to adopt individuals from *outside* his natural family, and give them a legal status of adoption, thus placing them *within* the family. Although a distinction would still be possible between the natural and adopted children, they have the same legal status in the eyes of the law, they are all members of the same family, irrespective of their origins. Paul uses this image to indicate that, through faith, believers come to have the same status as Jesus (as sons of God), without implying that they had the same divine nature as Jesus. Faith brings about a change in our status before God, incorporating us within the family of God, despite the fact that we do not share the same divine origins as Christ.

Secondly, it expresses the idea that the adopted children have the same inheritance rights as the natural son. The adopted children are entitled to receive the same inheritance as the natural son. Paul points out that the inheritance which Jesus received from his father is suffering and glory. Christians may expect to receive the same from his hand. 'Now if we are children, then we are heirs – heirs of God and co-heirs with Christ, if indeed we share in his sufferings in order that we may also share in his glory' (Romans 8:17). In other words, resurrection and eternal life are the inheritance of Christians (1 Peter 1:3–4). What Jesus obtained by his obedience will one day be ours. He is the 'firstfruits' of the dead

(1 Corinthians 15:20–23): that is, the first of a rich harvest (for the idea of 'firstfruits', see Exodus 23:16). Christ has been raised; we shall be raised, as those who share in him. In thinking of the resurrection of Christ, we are actually looking ahead to our own resurrection on the last day.

But what of 'life everlasting', the Creed's old-fashioned way of speaking about 'eternal life'? Having affirmed that we will one day share Christ's resurrection, the Creed now hints at what form our existence will take. The idea of 'eternal life' might seem to suggest little more than life that goes on and on and on. Doesn't that sound terribly boring? It probably does, if you think of eternal life as an infinite extension of our present lives. But that isn't really what is meant. The Greek language, in which the New Testament is written, has two words for life. One (*bios*) means 'mere biological existence'; the other (*zoē*) means 'life in all its fullness'. What we are being offered is fullness of life (John 10:10), which not even death itself can destroy. We are not being offered an endless extension of our biological existence, but rather a transformation of that existence. 'Eternal' doesn't mean throughout all time; it means outside time. 'Eternal life' means 'life with God, outside the confines of space and time'. As it is virtually impossible for us to conceive what it must be like to live outside space and time, it is understandably difficult to think about eternal life. However, the main point is this: eternal life means that our present relationship with God is not destroyed or thwarted by death, but is continued and deepened by it.

However, we must not think of eternal life as something which lies totally in the future. It is something that we can begin to experience now. It is certainly true that eternal life, in all its fullness, is something we can only hope to gain in the age to come (Luke 18:30). Nevertheless, we are able to gain a foretaste of that eternal life now. Jesus' words to Martha (John 11:25–26), just before the raising of Lazarus, are especially important here. 'I am the resurrection and the life. He who believes in me will live, though he dies; and whoever lives and believes in me will never die.' In the first part of this statement, Jesus declares that anyone who believes in him will come to life – a life which is not terminated by death itself.

In the second, however, he proclaims that whoever believes in him will come to life in such a way that death cannot cancel it. To believe is to be born again, to come to newness of life which endures for ever and ever. To come to faith in Jesus Christ is to begin a new relationship with God which is not abolished by death, but which is actually deepened – death sweeps away the remaining obstacles to our experiencing the presence of God. This is not to say that our resurrection has already taken place (2 Timothy 2:18); it is to say that we may catch a glimpse of what eternal life is like here and now. Eternal life is inaugurated, but not fulfilled, in our present life as believers. To enter fully into eternal life is not to experience something totally strange and unknown. Rather, it is to extend and deepen our experience of the presence and love of God.

Finally, note that the Creed ends with a single word: 'Amen.' This reminds us that the Creed is as much a prayer as a statement of faith. It is a prayer for deepening our faith in and commitment to the God whose greatness we have just considered. To say 'Amen!' to the Creed is to pray that the power and presence of God might touch our lives, deepen our love for him, and enhance our understanding of his gospel. Earlier (pp. 18–24) we saw that faith involves more than assent – it involves trust and obedience. The Creed will have done its job, and done it well, if it propels us out into God's world, determined to serve him with the same faithfulness and dedication as those who first used this Creed, all those centuries ago.

The ideas applied

Everyone lives in hope. In fact, without hope for the future, life can be unbearable. One of the most poignant recent explorations of the importance of hope may be found in Nevil Shute's novel *On the Beach*. A nuclear war has devastated the northern hemisphere. Australians, initially unaffected, gradually realize that they will be wiped out by the radioactive fallout that is drifting their way. The situation is hopeless. With great insight, Shute explores the way in which humans respond to a hopeless situation. Many of them deny what is going to happen. 'There's *got* to be hope', cries one of the characters, as she desperately seeks assurance that all will be well.

Many people instinctively feel this way in the face of death and extinction. There's *got* to be hope. Yet nothing on earth seems able to provide it. Here the Christian proclamation of resurrection and eternal life is of crucial importance. It is not just that it is true; it is also of urgent relevance to human existence. It meets a vital human need. It is important that the Christian hope gets a hearing in today's world. 'Always be prepared to give an answer to everyone who asks you to give the reason for the hope that you have' (1 Peter 3:15). Evangelism and personal witness are of critical importance. Your lifestyle – the attitudes you adopt to life and death – can proclaim your firm grasp of the Christian hope as well as, if not better than, any words you might use.

Remember that the English word 'hope' is ambiguous. 'I hope it won't rain', means 'It would be very nice if it didn't rain (but I have a sinking feeling it will).' That is hope in its weak sense – a faint and forlorn wish. But there is a strong sense of the word. Hope, in its full-blooded sense, means 'a sure and confident expectation'. The Christian hope is indeed confident and assured. To 'put our hope in the living God' (1 Timothy 4:10) is to look to him in confidence and trust, knowing and relying upon his faithfulness and constancy. It is this hope which has inspired Christian endurance down the ages (1 Thessalonians 1:3). And it is this same hope which can sustain you in times of joy and sorrow.

Finally, as we bring this study of the Creed to an end, remember that we have not been dealing with ideas, but with the living God. To wrestle with the Creed is to fathom the wonders of God's saving love for us, as we trace the story of Jesus Christ and its implications for us. The Creed must be allowed to touch our hearts as much as to inform our minds – and to prepare us for the day on which we shall stand in the presence and power of God.

Key scriptural passages

John 11: 21–27; 1 Corinthians 15; Revelation 21:1 – 22:6.

Questions for discussion

Is it helpful to distinguish 'resurrection' and 'eternal life'? Or are they just two sides of the same coin?

How would you explain the idea of 'eternal life' to a non-believer?

What does it mean to 'hope in God'? (See Psalms 130:7; 146:5; 147:11; Isaiah 40:31; 1 Timothy 6:17).

For further reading

Ray S. Anderson, *Theology, Death and Dying*, pp. 82–123. A fine account of Christian views on hope, written mainly with the needs of an academic public in mind.

Brian Hebblethwaite, *The Christian Hope*. An excellent survey of its field. Well within the grasp of the educated layperson.

Steven Travis, *The Jesus Hope*. A splendid, lucid and readable guide to this important theme. Highly recommended.

Bibliography

Anderson, J. N. D., *The Mystery of the Incarnation* (London: Hodder & Stoughton, 1978).

Anderson, Ray S., *Theology, Death and Dying* (Oxford/ New York: Basil Blackwell, 1986).

Bray, Gerald, *Creeds, Councils and Christ* (Leicester: Inter-Varsity Press, 1984).

Bruce, F. F., *The Real Jesus* (London: Hodder & Stoughton, 1985).

Chadwick, Henry, *The Early Church* (Harmondsworth: Penguin, 1982).

France, R. T., *The Evidence for Jesus* (London: Hodder & Stoughton, 1986).

—, *The Living God* (London: Inter-Varsity Press, 1970).

Green, E. M. B., *I believe in the Holy Spirit* (London: Hodder & Stoughton, 1975).

—, *The Day Death Died* (Leicester: Inter-Varsity Press, 1982).

—, *The Empty Cross of Jesus* (London: Hodder & Stoughton, 1984).

Guinness, Os, *Doubt: Faith in Two Minds* (Tring: Lion, 1979).

Hebblethwaite, Brian, *The Christian Hope* (Basingstoke: Marshall Pickering, 1984).

Hengel, Martin, *Crucifixion* (London: SCM Press, 1976).
Houston, James, *I believe in the Creator* (London: Hodder & Stoughton, 1979).
Hughes, P. E., *The True Image: The Origin and Destiny of Man in Christ* (Leicester: Inter-Varsity Press, 1989).
Jackman, David, *Understanding the Church* (Eastbourne: Kingsway Publications, 1987).
Kelly, J. N. D., *Early Christian Creeds* (London: Longmans, 1950).
Kreeft, Peter, *Making Sense out of Suffering* (London: Hodder & Stoughton, 1986).
Küng, Hans, *The Church* (London: Search Press, 1968).
Lewis, C. S., *Mere Christianity* (London: Collins, many reprints).
—, *The Problem of Pain* (London: Collins, many reprints).
—, *The Great Divorce* (London: Collins, many reprints).
McGrath, Alister E., *Understanding Jesus* (Eastbourne: Kingsway, 1986).
—, *Understanding the Trinity* (Eastbourne: Kingsway, 1986).
—, *Explaining Your Faith* (Leicester: Inter-Varsity Press, 1988).
—, *Doubt: Handling it honestly* (Leicester: Inter-Varsity Press, 1990).
—, *A Cloud of Witnesses: Ten Great Christian Thinkers* (Leicester: Inter-Varsity Press, 1990).
Morris, Leon, *The Apostolic Preaching of the Cross* (Grand Rapids: Eerdmans, 1965).
Neill, Stephen, *The Supremacy of Jesus* (London: Hodder & Stoughton, 1984).

Packer, J. I., *Knowing God* (London: Hodder & Stoughton, 1975).
Ramsey, Michael, *Holy Spirit* (London: SPCK, 1977).
Ryle, J. C., *Holiness* (Welwyn: Evangelical Press, 1979).
Schaeffer, Francis A., *True Spirituality* (Wheaton, Ill.: Tyndale Press, 1971).
Smail, Tom, *Reflected Glory* (London: Hodder & Stoughton, 1987).
Stott, J. R. W., *The Cross of Christ* (Leicester: Inter-Varsity Press, 1986).
Tidball, Derek, *Skilful Shepherds: An Introduction to Pastoral Theology* (Leicester: Inter-Varsity Press, 1986).
Travis, Stephen H., *The Jesus Hope* (Leicester: Inter-Varsity Press, 1980).
Watson, David, *I believe in the Church* (London: Hodder & Stoughton, 1978).
Webster, Jonathan, *God is here! Believing in the Incarnation Today* (Basingstoke: Marshall, Morgan and Scott, 1983).
Wiersbe, Warren, *Why Us? When Bad Things Happens to God's People* (Leicester: Inter-Varsity Press, 1980).

Doubt
Handling it honestly
ALISTER McGRATH

Doubt can be a good thing! Writing with insight and sensitivity, Alister McGrath explores what doubt is, and how it can lead to real spiritual growth. Many doubts and anxieties which Christians have about their faith are explored clearly, concisely and convincingly. This book is packed with helpful illustrations and practical suggestions. It is a vital and long-awaited resource for those troubled by doubt – or wishing to help their doubting friends.

Alister McGrath is widely regarded as an outstanding and creative Christian communicator of the late twentieth century. His previous books include *Explaining Your Faith* (IVP), *Understanding Jesus* and *Understanding the Trinity* (Kingsway). He teaches at Wycliffe Hall, Oxford, and is married with two children.

'One of the major younger theologians in England . . . a superb communicator.'
Church Times

'A brilliant communicator.' *Anvil*

144 pages *Pocketbook*

Inter-Varsity Press

Explaining Your Faith
(without losing your friends)
ALISTER McGRATH

You want to tell your non-Christian friends how exciting and relevant Christianity is. But what do you say?

Christian faith looks very different from the outside looking in! How can you explain it so that it makes sense to your friends?

Alister McGrath's book provides a straightforward, readable and intelligible account of what Christians believe – and why they believe it. He takes key topics that often come up in discussions, and shows how to explain them clearly.

112 pages *Pocketbook*

Inter-Varsity Press

A Cloud of Witnesses
Ten great Christian thinkers
ALISTER McGRATH

This book presents key ideas of ten leading Christian thinkers, along with information about their lives and times which helps to bring them alive as individuals. You will be able to see why many of them set the world afire, as their ideas kindled a response in passing from mind to mind.

Each of the thinkers casts light on a theme that a student beginning to study theology is likely to encounter. People such as Martin Luther, John Calvin or C. S. Lewis will stimulate and inform your own thinking about a variety of topics – such as the meaning of grace, our knowledge of God in Scripture and nature, and the human longing for God.

160 pages *'B' format*

Pocket Guide to Christian Beliefs

I. HOWARD MARSHALL

★ *how* we can know about God
★ *what* we can know about God
★ who Jesus is
★ what Jesus did
★ living the Christian life
★ the Christian community
★ Jesus' return
★ life after death

Here is a book which will bring growth and joy to your Christian faith and life. With its questions for study and discussion, it is ideal for new Christians and those who want a refresher course.

144 pages *Pocketbook*

Inter-Varsity Press